Professor Pincushion's
Beginner Guide to Sewing

Garment Making for Nervous Newbies

> I think she's talking about me!

Tova Opatrny

stash BOOKS®

an imprint of C&T Publishing

Text copyright © 2022 by Tova Opatrny

Photography provided and paid for by C&T Publishing copyright © 2022 by C&T Publishing

Photography provided by Tova Opatrny copyright © 2022 by Tova Opatrny

Publisher: Amy Barrett-Daffin

Creative Director: Gailen Runge

Acquisitions Editor: Roxane Cerda

Editor: Madison Moore

Technical Editor: Helen Frost

Cover/Book Designer: April Mostek

Production Coordinator: Zinnia Heinzmann

Illustrators: Casey Dukes, Mary E. Flynn

Photography Coordinator: Lauren Herberg

Photography Assistant: Gabriel Martinez

Front cover illustration by Casey Dukes

Subjects and lifestyle photography by Lauren Herberg of C&T Publishing, Inc.; instructional photography by Tova Opatrny, unless otherwise noted

Published by Stash Books, an imprint of C&T Publishing, Inc., P.O. Box 1456, Lafayette, CA 94549

Attention Teachers: C&T Publishing, Inc., encourages the use of our books as texts for teaching. You can find lesson plans for many of our titles at ctpub.com or contact us at ctinfo@ctpub.com.

We take great care to ensure that the information included in our products is accurate and presented in good faith, but no warranty is provided, nor are results guaranteed. Having no control over the choices of materials or procedures used, neither the author nor C&T Publishing, Inc., shall have any liability to any person or entity with respect to any loss or damage caused directly or indirectly by the information contained in this book. For your convenience, we post an up-to-date listing of corrections on our website (ctpub.com). If a correction is not already noted, please contact our customer service department at ctinfo@ctpub.com or P.O. Box 1456, Lafayette, CA 94549.

Trademark (™) and registered trademark (®) names are used throughout this book. Rather than use the symbols with every occurrence of a trademark or registered trademark name, we are using the names only in the editorial fashion and to the benefit of the owner, with no intention of infringement.

Library of Congress Cataloging-in-Publication Data

Names: Opatrny, Tova, 1978- author.
Title: Professor Pincushion's beginner guide to sewing : garment making for nervous newbies / Tova Opatrny.
Description: Lafayette, CA : Stash Books, an imprint of C&T Publishing, Inc., [2022] | Includes index. | Summary: "Professor Pincushion's Beginner Guide to Sewing is part textbook, part how-to, and all cheeky fun. Follow along with information on sewing tools and supplies, how to read commercial patterns and sewing techniques commonly used in garment sewing. Inside are five projects perfect for new and skilled sewers"-- Provided by publisher"-- Provided by publisher.
Identifiers: LCCN 2022021439 | ISBN 9781644032428 (trade paperback) | ISBN 9781644032435 (ebook)
Subjects: LCSH: Sewing.
Classification: LCC TT712 .O65 2022 | DDC 646--dc23/eng/20220601
LC record available at https://lccn.loc.gov/2022021439

Printed in the USA

10 9 8 7 6 5 4 3 2 1

Dedication

This book is dedicated to the viewers of Professor Pincushion for their support and love.

And to The Professor's Assistant who's never been afraid to walk this rambling, wild path with me from the very beginning.

Acknowledgments

The Professor Pincushion channel has never been a solo endeavor and neither was this book.

First, a huge thanks to my agent, Ashley Blake, who's become a force at getting my words out there in the world.

Thanks to all the companies who generously provided supplies: Ashley Guido at Brother Sewing Machine, Kelly Morris and Chrissy Solomon at Riley Blake Designs, Paula Layton at Dritz, Holly Vlasak at Fiskars, Shivanthi Vannan and David Briganti at Rowenta, Tammy Russo at Design Group Americas for Simplicity Patterns and McCall's Patterns, and Lynn Brown at Coats & Clark.

The people behind the scenes played such a big role in taking my words and actually making them into something special. Thanks to Jenn DeShazer for pattern grading. And a big thanks to the whole team at C&T Publishing: Roxane Cerda, Liz Aneloski, Madison Moore, and the rest of the amazing crew. Also, thanks to Casey Dukes and April Mostek for bringing Pinny and friends to life. Thanks for making my dream come true.

I wouldn't be where I am without the love of family and friends who encouraged me when Professor Pincushion was barely a channel. My parents always told me I could do anything, but without their support, it would have been a lot harder. And, of course, The Professor's Assistant, thank you. I'm sorry I couldn't sneak in more Highlander references, but there can be only one. Love you.

Contents

So You Want to Learn How to Sew Clothes ... An Introduction by Professor Pincushion 6

Chapter One: Tools and Supplies **8**

Sewing Tools 9

Supplies 15

Chapter Two: The Sewing Machine **18**

Choosing a Sewing Machine 19

Sewing Machine Safety 20

Anatomy of a Sewing Machine 20

Let's Practice! 25

Let's Thread! 27

Changing the Needle and Presser Foot 33

Chapter Three: Fabric **34**

Fabric Stores 36

Woven and Knit Fabric 38

Right Side and Wrong Side 40

Chapter Four: Fun with Knit Fabric **42**

Project Time: T-Shirt Upcycling 43

Project Time: T-Shirt Bag 46

Break Time: Needles 47

Chapter Five: Fun with Woven Fabric **50**

Project Time: Hair Scrunchie   51 ●●●●●●●●●▶

Break Time: Let's Learn About Seams   52

Break Time: Let's Thread a Hand Needle   55

Chapter Six: Intro to Patterns **60**

Lookbooks   62

Choosing a Pattern Size   64

Gathering Supplies   66

Chapter Seven: Working with Patterns **70**

Cutting Out Pattern Pieces   72

Downloadable Patterns   74

Treating Our Fabric Right   75

Putting Pattern Pieces to Fabric   76

Chapter Eight: Pajama Shorts **80**

Project Time: Pajama Shorts   81 ●●●●●

Break Time: I Don't Like My Seam!   83

Chapter Nine: T-Shirt **92**

●●●●● Project Time: T-Shirt   93

Break Time: Sleeves   95

Chapter Ten: Conclusion **108**

Index **110**

About the Author **111**

Photo by Allison Clarke

So You Want to Learn How to Sew Clothes ...
An Introduction by Professor Pincushion

Betsy Ross, American flag maker, was a huge influencer in her day. Before her, people wore plain garments made from boring fabrics—probably lots of brown and gray. Then Betsy came along, did her thing, and people said, "Whoa! What's this stripe thing going on? Are those stars?" Trust me, their minds were blown, and she got tons of social media likes … or whatever the equivalent was back in those days. At least, that's what I assume was the case. To be honest, I made this whole thing up in order to make a point about the power of sewing, and she was the most famous seamstress I could think of. Anyway, luckily for you, I'm not here to teach history. If you want to make like Betsy and blow people's minds using a needle and thread, you've come to the right place.

Betsy Ross (Influencer)

Jean Leon Gerome Ferris, Public domain, via Wikimedia Commons

Sewing your own clothes is fun and exciting and scary—or maybe it was just scary for me. I learned to sew in high school and everything about it terrified me, so I only made hair scrunchies for the longest time. Despite my initial lack of courage, I now know it's the best hobby for at least two reasons. Number one: When you strut down the street and someone asks about your outfit, you get to reply, "Oh, this? Yeah, I made it." And then watch their mouth pop open like a goldfish's. It's the best feeling in the world. The second reason, the most important one, is that you can make a garment that's completely you.

If you buy clothes in a store, your options are limited to availability. When you make your own clothes, you choose the style and the fabric, which gives you control over almost everything! It's the very definition of self-expression. If you're picturing a fully beaded ball gown with twenty layers of tulle, make it! If you want to show up at Comic-Con with the best Wonder Woman cosplay costume around, do it! Sewing dreams are today's inspiration for tomorrow's reality.

But I do have some bad news.

This book isn't going to give you directions for making an elaborate, goldfish-mouth-popping outfit because it's never a good idea to dive into the deep end of the sewing pool. Sewing requires patience, time, and skill.

But even the most complicated projects can be broken down into very basic elements. This book introduces sewing building blocks that will get you comfortable and develop skills that you'll continue to use as your sewing projects get more complex. Here's what my pal, Pinny the Straight Pin, says:

A stitch in time saves nine!

▶ **Confused?** This means it's better to take the time to do things correctly than to jump ahead haphazardly, which could lead to headaches … or tears. I'd say there's no crying in sewing, but my very damp pincushion proves otherwise. It's okay to get frustrated or make mistakes or cry into your pincushion. It's part of the learning process. But allow yourself to learn at a beginner's pace. You won't be perfect on day one.

The best news is that you will get better. Before you know it, you will be making amazing gowns or costumes. Think of it like collecting experience points (XP) in a game. You don't just start by taking on the biggest, baddest boss; instead, you, the hero, play through smaller quests to acquire tools and skills, gradually preparing yourself for harder challenges.

We need to collect our sewing XP.

XP powers my sewing to new levels

The more XP you collect, the more you'll gain an understanding of how clothes come together and, more importantly, why things are done in a certain way. This understanding makes it easier to sew complex items and to customize patterns for individual bodies.

▶ *Take a chance. Experiment!* Allow yourself to try new things. Just because we have to start at the beginning doesn't mean it won't be fun. Stick with Pinny and me, and every stitch will get you closer to your sewing dreams!

Chapter One
Tools and Supplies

It's important to start off on the right foot, which means the right tool in the right hand. Items can go into one of two categories: tools or supplies.

Sewing Tools

Tools are items used to help you sew, but are not part of the garment.

Huh?

▶ *Let's use Pinny as an example.* Straight pins are used when sewing a dress, but when the dress is finished there shouldn't be any straight pins left in it—at least, I would hope not. Ouch! Sewing tools can be used over and over again for each new project.

HERE ARE THE TOOLS YOU WILL NEED TO GET STARTED

Paper scissors	Needles	Iron and ironing board
Fabric scissors	Sewing gauge	
Straight pins	Flexible tape measure	Seam ripper
Pincushion	Fabric chalk, marker, or pencil	Sewing machine

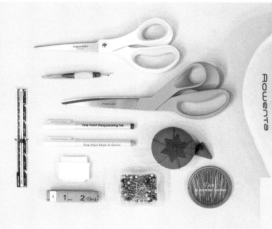

There are other, more specialized, sewing tools, but the ones on this list are the bare minimum and most often used.

Did you know the first scissors were made from the teeth of saber-toothed tigers?

Are there cookies in here or sewing tools? If your grandma sews, it could go either way.

▶ *Not true.* But Pinny brings up a good point. Sewing tool technology hasn't changed much over the years. This means you can borrow sewing tools from people, like your grandma, rather than buying them new.

Let's break down each tool.

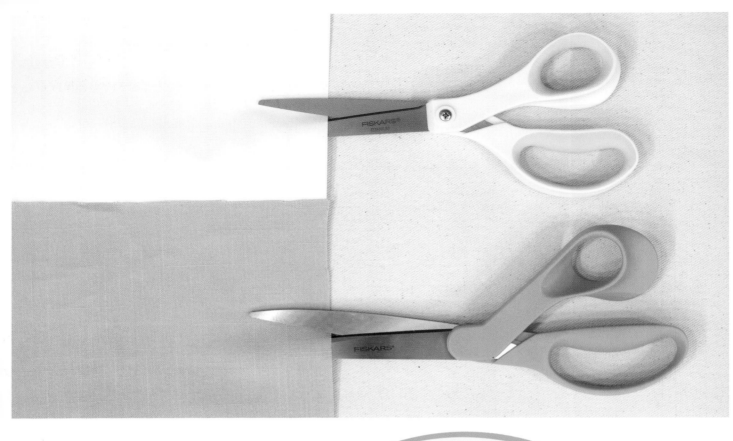

Scissors

Scissors are one of the most important sewing tools. You'll be cutting patterns, fabric, notches, and threads. Phew! Lots of cutting. It's almost as if you should own *two* pairs of scissors. Ha! Wouldn't that be hilarious? Two pairs of scissors. Actually, you should have two pairs of scissors. Cutting paper will eventually dull scissor blades, and you've never known frustration like trying to cut fabric and watching it bend over the blades like a tortilla. Hence owning both paper scissors and fabric scissors.

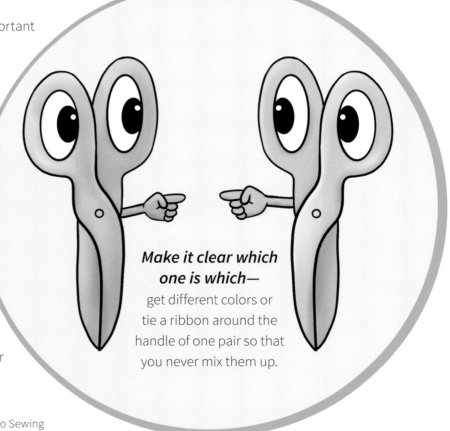

Make it clear which one is which— get different colors or tie a ribbon around the handle of one pair so that you never mix them up.

Straight Pins and a Pincushion

Straight pins help us hold fabric pieces together before they are sewn. The sharp point goes through the fabric and the other side has a colorful ball. Straight pins are a wonderful tool and they have a best friend. Any guesses?

▶ **It's the pincushion!**

We're pin-tastic!

Pinny should only be in two places, either in your fabric to help with sewing or hanging out in the sewing waiting room: the pincushion. Lonely straight pins should never be loose on the table or on the floor.

Best-friend pincushions can come in many different forms, from the traditional tomato to something you wear on your wrist like a bracelet or even a magnetic dish. Pins need to be stored safely. My grandma had a saying, "Pins go in the tomato and not in your foot." It's not real snappy, probably because it's hard to rhyme when you've stepped on a straight pin and need to go to the doctor to get it removed. Yeah, that happened to my grandma; please let that be a lesson for all of us.

Don't step on me!

Needles

Now you may be thinking, *"I have a sewing machine. Do I really need hand needles?"* ▶ **Yes, you do.** Next question. But seriously, hand sewing is done more often than you think. Like straight pins, they should also be stored correctly.

Sewing Gauge and Flexible Tape Measure

Let's go on an amazing ride called *Our Imagination.* After weeks of making the most amazing costume, you're ready to show the world. You pull on the garment and—wait, that can't be right. Why is it too tight in the shoulders and baggy around the waist? After all this work, your masterpiece is unwearable? Commence crying into the pincushion.

Because I like you, I'm going to share the greatest sewing secret of all. Come closer. Real close. Just press your face to the page because this is between you and me.

Hmm. I guess that's not much of a secret. Sorry if I just shouted into your eyeballs. But it's true. The best clothes are the ones that fit. And, in sewing, we don't guesstimate. We measure and then we measure again.

Measure accurately!

Two commonly used measuring tools are the sewing gauge and the flexible tape measure. The sewing gauge looks like a tiny ruler with a slider in the center, and it measures small areas of the garment. The flexible tape measure is an accessory we drape over our shoulders because it's hip and trendy.

Working it!

Robert Kneschke/Shutterstock.com

▶ *Okay, that's not true.* The flexible tape measure is mainly used for taking body measurements to figure out garment sizing (sewing patterns use a different sizing system than department store clothes).

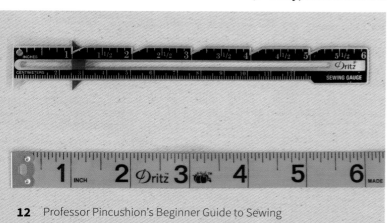

Did you know you can draw on fabric? It's true!

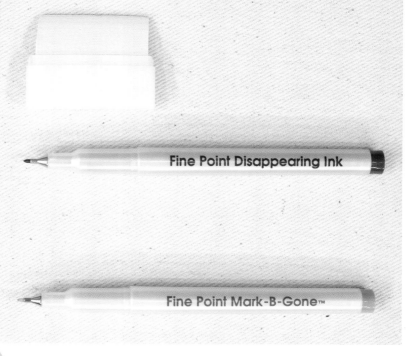

Fine Point Disappearing Ink

Fine Point Mark-B-Gone™

I'm making zee masterpiece.

Fabric Chalk, Marker, or Pencil

Don't get too excited because we're not making art. These marks are used to help us match pieces together. You'll need a fabric marker, pencil, or chalk. Although variety is best. You may think white fabric chalk works great; that is, until you work with white fabric, making your marks invisible. We don't like invisible marks because then we're guessing. Remember, guessing can lead to crying, and no one wants to cry.

Iron and Ironing Board

The iron is a sewing MVP. You may have used an iron to remove wrinkles in your clothes. But in sewing, we use an iron to *press*, or flatten, fabric. You'll be pressing almost as much as you'll be sewing. Why do we do so much pressing? It helps with accuracy. If the fabric is a wrinkled mess, chances are it's going to be harder for you to be accurate with things like seams and measurements.

Note: Being careless and burning yourself on a hot iron is almost as bad as stepping on pins. Please be careful.

Are you imPRESSed with my abilities?

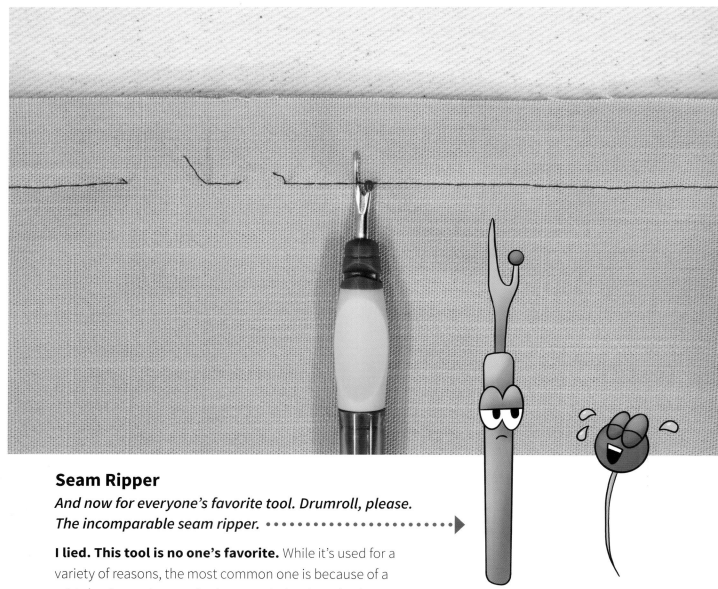

Seam Ripper

And now for everyone's favorite tool. Drumroll, please. The incomparable seam ripper. •••••••••••••••••••••••►

I lied. This tool is no one's favorite. While it's used for a variety of reasons, the most common one is because of a mistake. Seam rippers: ripping out stitches but also hearts.

Professor Pincushion uses the seam ripper all the time

►*I beg your pardon.* I don't use it *all* the time. Maybe I did yesterday and that time last week and … you know what, I don't think we really need to go into it. Let's just say I'm quite familiar with the process. Plus, there's nothing wrong with making mistakes. It happens. Good news: most sewing mistakes can be fixed. Getting another chance to get it right wouldn't be possible without the seam ripper.

Supplies

Supplies are the fun items that a garment is made of. There are two categories: fabric and notions.

Fabric

The fabric category includes fabric, lining, and interfacing; basically any fabric-type material. Fabric is the foundation of the whole garment. Without it, you're stitching air. When clothes are invisible, no one sees your mistakes … but they will see everything else. **Ooh la la.**

Fabric comes in all different types and can be bought at your local fabric store on rolls, called *bolts*. Buying fabric can be the most fun part of this hobby. This is why many sewists have a "stash," a.k.a. a pile of fabric created when you buy fabric without a plan in mind. Or when you save fabric scraps because maybe that 2″ rectangle can be used again later. Regardless of the reason, it can happen to you.

You'll never find me fabric booty!

eAlisa/Shutterstock.com

But you can use this information to your advantage if you have family or friends who sew. Sewing isn't a cheap hobby, which pushes you to be creative about where to get your supplies. When starting out, reach out to this experienced sewing person in your life. First, butter them up by telling them you admire the height of their stash and appreciate their fine taste. Then drop the hint that you are also learning to sew. Sewists are a very generous group, and they may donate to the cause. Free fabric is the best fabric.

When the fabric cutter asks if you have a big project but all you're doing is adding to your stash

If you don't know anyone with a stash and don't have a lot of money to spend on fabric, you may find some at a thrift store or you can use bedsheets and old clothes. You can also save buttons or zippers from old garments to be reused again. (In this case, the seam ripper will be used as a force for good.) Fabric possibilities are all around you.

But make sure you have permission before cutting anything that is not yours. Causing a family rift by slicing up Grandma's heirloom quilt might necessitate you entering the Witness Protection Program.

New pincushion. Who dis?

Notions

Notions are everything else you'll need for your garment. This includes buttons, thread, zippers, trim, and elastic. All projects will have at least one notion—thread—because you can't sew without it. But consult your pattern to see if you need anything else. You don't want to start a new project and then realize you forgot to buy buttons.

There are many options when it comes to thread. When in doubt, all-purpose thread will work for most projects. Try matching thread color to fabric color. (In this book, I'll be using a contrasting thread color so it's easier to see.) Avoid old thread. If Grandma hands you a bag of thread that's been around for twenty years, thank her and then throw it away. When fibers get old, they get fragile. You don't want to spend your time sewing clothes and then watch your seams fall apart.

I don't want a wardrobe malfunction!

▶ *Congratulations, you made it through Chapter One!*
You now have a good foundation of supply knowledge. Let's keep leveling up and tackle the biggest sewing tool of all: the sewing machine.

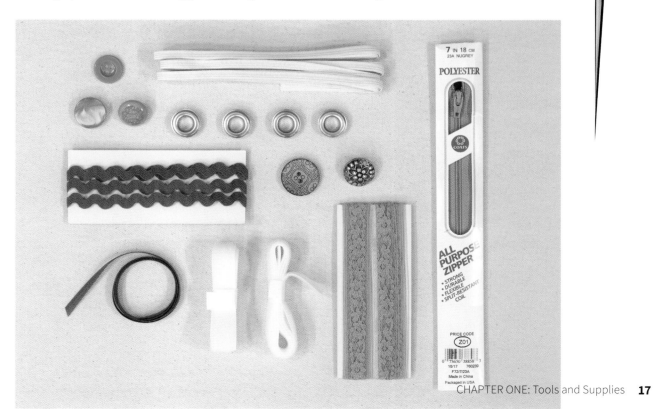

Chapter Two

The Sewing Machine

If you looked at the title, felt your stomach shrivel inside your body, and are thinking, "Isn't there another topic we can cover?" take a breath. Pinny and I are here for you, and we're going to conquer this machine together. After a little bit of practice, it might become your new best friend (that you occasionally call a bad name).

> *I'm scary but friendly.*

▶ **What is a sewing machine?** Unfortunately, the answer is not a machine that can make a pair of pants at the push of a button. Instead, a sewing machine is an important tool that can help in the construction of a garment. When you press the foot pedal, the needle loops thread in the upper part of the machine with thread in the lower part of the machine. Every time these threads loop together, you get a stitch.

Choosing a Sewing Machine

Sewing newbies always ask, "What's the best sewing machine I can buy?" The best machine means the best results, right?

> *I deserve ALL the bells and whistles.*

But sewing machines can cost anywhere from less than $100 to several thousands of dollars.

> *YIKES! Maybe I'll take some bells, no whistle.*

▶ **Good news!** You don't need a $5,000 Cadillac sewing machine. In fact, it's sometimes better to buy a simpler machine so it's easier to figure out how to use it. While fancy sewing machines can be fun, most of the time you'll only be sewing a straight stitch and the occasional zigzag or buttonhole stitch. You can make amazing clothes with a basic machine and upgrade to something better if needed.

If money is tight, check thrift stores for a used machine. Before using, it should be taken into your local sewing machine shop for maintenance. Repeat maintenance once a year, for all machines, to keep them in good working order.

Sewing Machine Safety

It's important to learn how to use a sewing machine correctly and safely. You don't want to damage the machine, and you also don't want to hurt yourself. Bloodstains can ruin a garment's aesthetic.

Sewing machine rule number one is very simple:

The sewing machine stays off until you're actually sewing.

The biggest thing people are afraid of is getting a needle through the finger. Taking the proper precautions makes the chance of this happening slim. When the sewing machine is on, always be aware of your hands, and keep them away from the needle. Sewists can create beauty without pain … at least without the physical kind, and emotional pain can be treated with a bowl of ice cream or two.

Anatomy of a Sewing Machine

Sewing machines all work essentially the same way, even if appearances vary from machine to machine. If you get good at using one sewing machine, you can move on to another one fairly easily.

I'm going to be going over some basic parts of a sewing machine, but since yours might look slightly different, you should consult your manual too. And don't feel like you need to memorize everything right away because you'll get familiar with the different parts as you begin to use them more. Let's do this.

This Brother CP60X is a thing of beauty.

The Handwheel and Power Switch

First, look at the *handwheel*, the big knob on the right side of the machine. If you turn this knob toward you, the needle will go up and down. You're already sewing manually, although I don't recommend sewing like this. It would take forever.

Sewing newbies may sometimes turn the handwheel in the wrong direction, away from them.

No one tells me what to do.

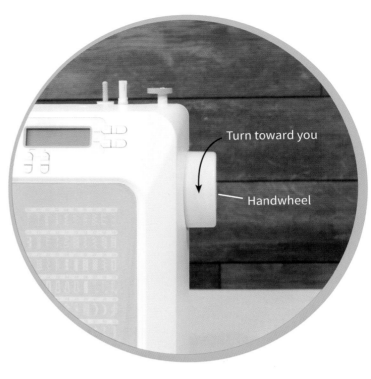

Turn toward you

Handwheel

Will turning the handwheel backward break the machine? ▶ **No**, but it isn't good for it, so get in the habit of only turning it toward you.

On/off switch

Foot controller jack

Power supply jack

Beneath the handwheel is the machine's **on/off switch**, power supply jack for plugging in the machine, and foot controller jack for plugging in the foot pedal. After the foot pedal is plugged in, it goes on the floor and is used like a gas pedal to control the speed of the stitching.

Spool Pin and Bobbin Pin

At the top of the machine, you might find two plastic or metal pins. The longer one is the **thread spool pin**. The thread spool pin could also be a horizontal pin on the back or front of the machine. Don't forget to check your manual. The small pin is the **bobbin winder pin**. Don't stress out if you don't know what a bobbin is yet.

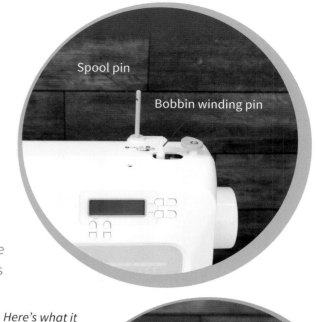

Spool pin

Bobbin winding pin

Front Panel

You might have a few dials or buttons on the front of the machine. Included here is the **stitch length**, which tells you how long the individual stitches are.

Stitch width determines how far the needle moves horizontally in between stitches. If you're doing a straight stitch, this dial will be at zero. The more you increase the number, the more you'll get a stitch that looks like a zigzag.

Stitch selector allows you to choose different types of stitches. Sometimes it's as simple as pushing a button or turning a dial, but consult your manual to find out the specifics, and experiment on scrap fabric.

Here's what it might look like on a computerized machine.

Stitch length

Stitch width

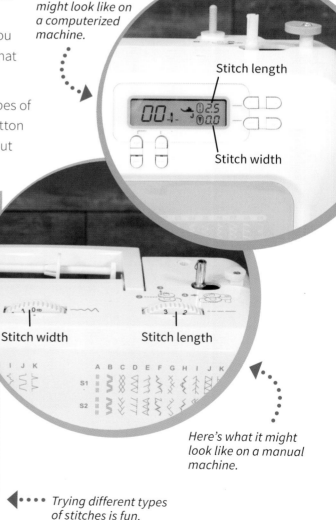

Stitch width

Stitch length

Here's what it might look like on a manual machine.

Trying different types of stitches is fun.

Thread Tension Dial

The **thread tension dial** controls how tightly the upper and lower threads loop together. This should be adjusted depending on the fabric. For my machine, the thicker the fabric, the higher the thread tension needed. If thread tension is too high, the fabric will pucker or threads might break. If the tension is too low, the stitches may appear loose. For our purposes, keep this number in the middle of the road, between 3 and 5.

Tension dial

Reverse Stitch

For sewing backward, use the **reverse stitch (or backstitch) lever or button**. This is on the front of the machine and commonly marked with a symbol that looks like a U-turn.

Use this button to stitch backward.

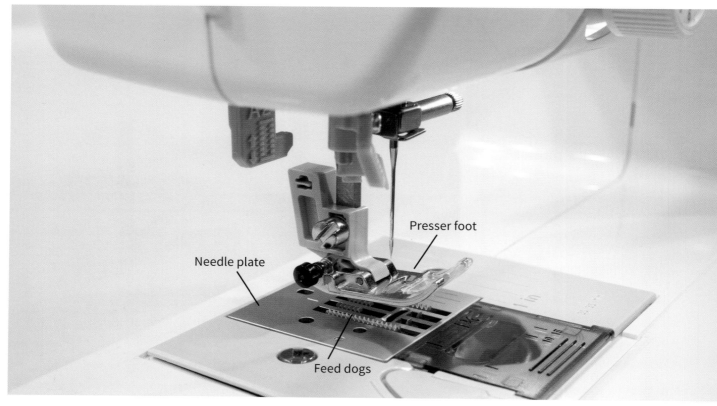

Presser Foot and Feed Dogs

Under the needle is the **presser foot**. This holds the fabric in place so we don't have to endanger our fingers. It also helps the **feed dogs**, the jagged teeth in the center of the **needle plate**, move the fabric. The presser foot can be changed out for different types of jobs. For now, we'll use the standard one.

The lever to raise and lower the presser foot should be on the back or the side of the machine. Try it for yourself. Presser foot goes up. Hey, we can put fabric underneath it. Presser foot goes down. Now we can start sewing. The presser foot must be down to sew.

But what about the bobbin? And all the slots on the machine?

▶ **Don't worry, Pinny!** We're going to get to those things, but let's take a break and practice using the parts we just talked about.

Let's Practice!

Download and print the Sewing Practice Sheet:

SCAN THIS QR CODE OR VISIT
tinyurl.com/11504-pattern1-download
to access the practice sheet. If you can't print it,
draw the lines on a blank piece of paper.

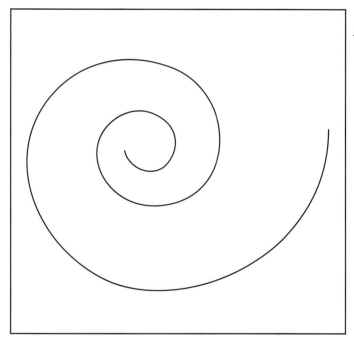

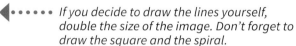 *If you decide to draw the lines yourself, double the size of the image. Don't forget to draw the square and the spiral.*

For this activity, you don't need your sewing machine to be threaded.

STEP 1 Raise the presser foot and needle, slip the practice sheet underneath, and line the needle up with one of the square's corners. To test the accuracy of your alignment, turn the handwheel toward you, bringing the needle down. Make adjustments to the paper before the needle goes all the way through. Once it's perfect, continue turning the handwheel, bringing the needle all the way into the paper.

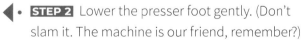 **STEP 2** Lower the presser foot gently. (Don't slam it. The machine is our friend, remember?)

STEP 3 Turn on your sewing machine. (Because it should have been *off* this whole time, newbies. That was a test!)

STEP 4 Plug in the foot pedal and place it on the floor where it's comfortable to reach with your foot. Step on the foot pedal slowly.

OMG!
It's moving!

▶ *Hey, look at you. You're doing it!* Guide the paper under the needle so that the needle is punching holes on the line. The paper should be moving under the presser foot on its own, allowing your hands to make small adjustments to keep the needle on target. Go as slow or as fast as you feel comfortable.

Oh no! I'm coming to a corner!

Breathe. *Before* getting to the corner, stop the machine by releasing the pressure on the foot pedal. Use the handwheel to manually sew forward until you're right on the corner. While the needle is down in the paper, raise the presser foot, rotate the paper so you can go in another direction, lower the presser foot, and then keep sewing. See if you can go around the whole square.

Need more practice? Print out another square and try again. This activity helps you learn to follow a line, practice accuracy, and get used to the sewing machine. When you're ready for more of a challenge, try the spiral on the printout. The more you practice, the better your accuracy will get.

With the needle down and the presser foot lifted, you can easily alter your sewing trajectory.

Let's Thread!

It's time to thread the sewing machine. Remember I said that a stitch is created when the machine loops together the upper and lower threads. So, it makes sense that threading happens in two parts: upper and lower.

Upper Threading

Let's tackle upper threading first. Many machines have arrows, numbers, or both showing the correct direction to thread.

To start, the needle and presser foot should be in the upright position, and the machine should be off. Put your spool of thread on the spool pin, pulling the thread so it unwinds across the front of the spool. Lead the thread to the first arrow, through the hook, called the *thread guide*, near the back of the machine.

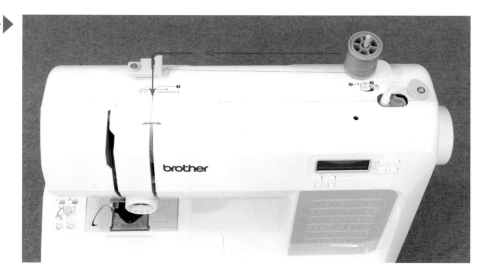

Take the thread, sliding it into the right slot on the front of the machine, known as the *thread channel*.

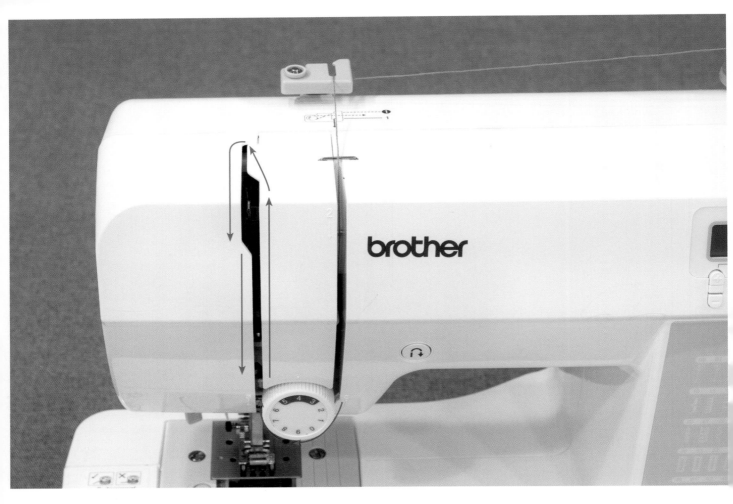

The thread goes to the bottom of this channel, going around the middle divide and up to the top of the left slot.

Inside the slot, there's a hook called the **thread take-up lever**.

If you can't see it, turn the handwheel toward you until it's in the highest position, and the lever should become visible.

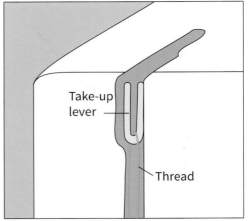

Take-up lever

Thread

Bring the thread to the right side of the hook, and then behind the hook. When you bring the thread forward again, it should slide into the hook, coming out on the left side of it.

The thread then goes back to the bottom of the left slot, toward the needle.

Above the needle is a horizontal hook, or thread guide. Pull the thread into the guide from right to left, above the hook.

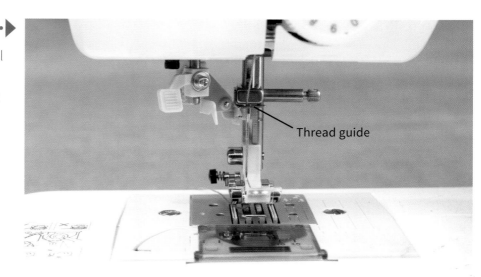

Thread guide

Finally, put the thread through the eye of the needle, usually going from front to back. After the thread is through the needle, it slips through the center of the presser foot and trails under it.

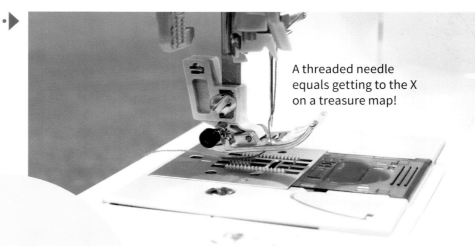

A threaded needle equals getting to the X on a treasure map!

Threading can vary from machine to machine, so definitely consult your manual. If stitches look off in some way, that can often be traced back to the threading. Always rethread the machine when troubleshooting.

Lower Threading

You're a whiz at threading the upper part of the machine. Now we're going to focus on the bobbin, which holds the thread for the lower half. Bobbins look like this:

Bobbins can be plastic or metal.

Sewing machines usually come with bobbins included, but you can buy additional ones too. Make sure to get the correct kind for your machine. There isn't a standard bobbin that works in all sewing machines. Sewing machines can either have a drop-in bobbin or front-loading bobbin.

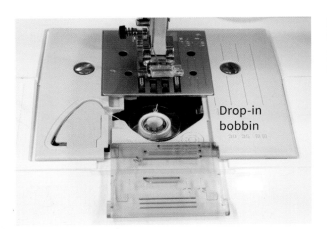

Drop-in bobbin

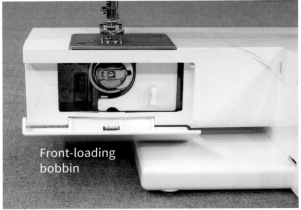

Front-loading bobbin

Bobbins don't come threaded, so you need to add thread from your spool. Put the thread spool on its pin. Unwind the thread, following the arrows for bobbin winding. On my machine, there are two arrows. One is for normal threading, and one is for the bobbin winding. I'll follow the one for bobbin winding, taking the thread clockwise around the metal disk before going toward the bobbin winding pin.

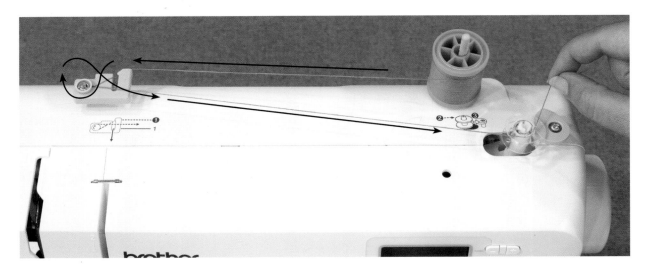

Some sewing machine bobbins have a tiny hole on the top of the bobbin. Put the thread through this hole and snap the bobbin onto the bobbin winder pin. Push the pin to the right to activate the bobbin-winding mode on the machine.

Keep hold of the thread coming from the hole until the bobbin starts to fill, otherwise the thread will come off the bobbin as it spins around. Press the foot pedal. The bobbin will start spinning and thread will wrap around it. The machine should fill the bobbin evenly on its own, but if the thread is stuck filling the same spot, lightly use a finger to gently guide the thread for even distribution.

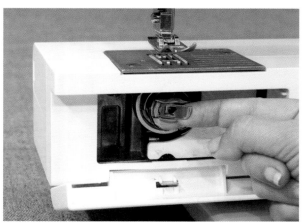

Once there's a good amount of thread, click the bobbin winding pin to the left, returning the machine to sewing mode. Cut the thread. The bobbin is ready to be used.

With a drop-in bobbin, slide the cover off and drop the bobbin in so that if you pull the thread, the bobbin turns counterclockwise. There will be arrows on the machine indicating where to put the thread. It will also be outlined in your manual. On my machine, I bring the thread to the metal plate at the front of the casing. Then, I slide the thread left into the break at the center of the plate.

If you have a front-loading bobbin, open the front bottom panel of the machine. Then remove the metallic casing by lifting the lever in the center of the casing and pulling out.

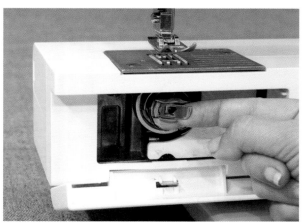

Your bobbin fits inside this casing. You'll notice there's a slit on the side of the casing; this is where you'll slide your thread through, pulling until the thread slips into the small hole. Check your manual for the correct direction of the thread.

Reinsert the casing into the machine until it clicks into place. Some of the bobbin thread should be hanging out of the machine.

Finish Threading

Now, it's time to bring the upper and lower threads together. Thread the upper part of the machine again (you can never have too much practice). After threading the needle, pull the thread until you have a 6″ tail. Hold this tail and turn the handwheel toward you. When the needle goes into the bottom of the machine it will catch the bobbin thread. Continue to turn the handwheel to bring the bobbin thread upward.

If you don't see it, gently pull upward on the upper thread tail and the bobbin thread should pop up from the center of the needle plate.

Pull the bobbin thread out, using a tool like your seam ripper to snag it. Make sure the machine is *off*. Once you have both tails, they should go under the presser foot.

▶ *Once both upper and lower threads are together under the presser foot, you're ready to start sewing!* Well, almost. There's one more thing I want to cover.

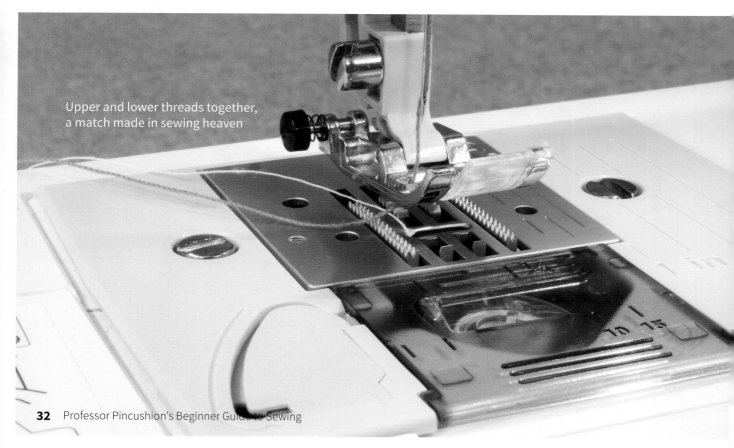

Upper and lower threads together, a match made in sewing heaven

Changing the Needle and Presser Foot

Paper can dull needles just like it dulls scissors. Since we practiced sewing on paper, that needle isn't ideal for sewing fabric. It's always a good idea to put a new needle in the machine before starting a new project. New needles are found in the notions department at your local fabric store and are chosen based on the type of fabric being sewn. We'll go over different needle types in Chapter Four (page 47).

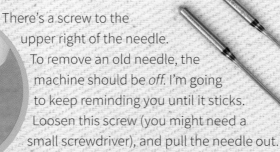

Needle screw

There's a screw to the upper right of the needle. To remove an old needle, the machine should be *off*. I'm going to keep reminding you until it sticks. Loosen this screw (you might need a small screwdriver), and pull the needle out.

One side of the top of the needle is flat. Insert the new needle; the flat part usually goes toward the back of the machine. Tighten the screw again, and you're ready to go.

If you ever need to change your presser foot, find the little lever right above the back of the foot. Push it in (or lift it), and the foot should come out. Use the lever again when inserting a new foot to lock it in place. Some machines don't have this lever and the foot merely pops in and out of its slot. Check your machine manual to know for sure.

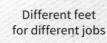
Different feet for different jobs

Now you're ready to sew!

Grab some scrap fabric and slide it under the foot, just like you did with the piece of paper. Start experimenting. Have fun and try different stitches.

Then, when you're ready, let's discuss fabric.

Chapter Three

Fabric

It's time to talk about my favorite subject: fabric. Why is fabric so wonderful? It's because there are so many types. Pretty, sparkly fabric! Soft, fuzzy fabric! Fabric with bears on it!

Oh my!

Bukhavets Mikhail/Shutterstock.com

You can choose fabric based on its print, texture, or type. It's really up to you. But before you go on a huge shopping spree and think this is a Wild West fabric free-for-all, let's take a breath.

I wouldn't reach for those pins if I were you, pardner.

▶ **Not all fabrics will work well in every situation,** so it's important to pick the right fabric for the project. No one's saying you can't use whatever fabric you want. Maybe you're excited for a pair of denim pajamas or a bomber jacket made from silk chiffon. But those denim pajamas are going to be uncomfortable to sleep in. That cool bomber jacket is going to lie flat and lifeless.

So how do I pick the right fabric?!

▶ **Where should you start?** Can you start sewing if you don't know the difference between satin and taffeta? If you cry in the store, will you get kicked out for blowing your nose into a bolt of fabric? Um, probably yes on that last question. Luckily, we're here to help.

Fabric Stores

Fabric stores are organized in a specific way. The floor layout is usually separated into three categories: **quilting/craft, apparel,** and **home decorating.** Your project will fall into one of these categories. When looking for fabric, the first question you should ask yourself is:

What am I making?

▶ *If you're making clothes, also known as apparel, start there.* Does this mean you should never look in the quilting or home decorating sections? I'm not one to use the word *never*. But to make it easy for beginners, let's keep things simple. Once you're in the right section, the next question you should be asking yourself is:

Casual or formal?

▶ *Will the garment be everyday streetwear or something fancy?* If it's the latter, check the *special occasion* section for lace, satin, velvet, or chiffon—all those nice, luxurious fabrics. If the apparel is casual, look at the apparel fabric outside the special occasion section. You'll find fabrics like denim, jersey knit, shirting, flannel, and corduroy.

After that, decide what kind of structure the garment should have. This is called **drape**, as in: How will the fabric drape on the body? Will the garment be soft and flowy? Does the fabric need to stretch? Sometimes this is easy to answer and sometimes it's more difficult.

I'm feeling overwhelmed again!

▶ *Luckily, there are products that can help us.* Commercial patterns (prepackaged instructions that go step-by-step through sewing a specific item) recommend specific fabric types and amounts. We'll get into using commercial patterns in Chapter Six (page 60). If you're really stuck on which fabric to get, chat with one of the sales associates at the store.

One problem sewists might be faced with is the temptation to choose a fabric because it calls to you like a sorceress, bewitching you with its beauty.

Look into my eyes and buy me!

▶ *Yes, that beautiful sequined fabric with the lace motif is just asking to be snatched up.* But this can be an expensive mistake. Not all fabrics are beginner friendly. You'll want to work your way up to challenging fabrics. Otherwise, the only thing you'll do with that expensive fabric is turn it into a giant handkerchief to blow your nose on.

All the fabrics suggested in this book are beginner fabrics. Save that beautiful sequined fabric for your "someday" pile. See? You're already starting to build a fabric stash. Excellent, my pupils. You're quickly learning the ways of The Professor.

Woven and Knit Fabric

No matter which department a fabric is found in, most fabrics will typically fall into one of two categories: woven or knit. This classification describes how the fibers in the fabric were put together. Fibers in woven fabric are interlaced together at 90° angles, like a basket. In knit fabric, the fibers interlock in loops, like the pattern of a sweater. This has nothing to do with the fabric content (that is, what the fibers are made of). For example, both woven and knit fabrics can be cotton.

Which type you pick depends on your project. You'll still refer to the fabric store questions from earlier, but this takes you another step forward.

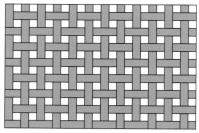

Woven

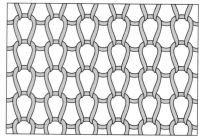

Knit

Woven Fabric

Let's start with woven fabric. What's great about it? There are tons of cute prints! It can be casual or fancy; there's a huge variety of types! You don't have to worry about it stretching while sewing with it! Denim, satin, chiffon, silk, velvet, and flannel are some popular woven fabrics.

What don't we like about woven fabric? It frays! And not just a random thread coming loose. Oh no, no, no, dear, sweet innocent newbies. Sometimes the edge of a woven fabric looks like a wooly mammoth in need of a haircut. It looks sloppy, and it can cause issues.

I call this work of art *The Fraying*. • • • • • • • • • ▶

Also, like I mentioned, woven fabric doesn't have much stretch. This is a positive when sewing, but if the garment you're making requires stretchiness, it's a problem. For instance, let's say you want to make something like a T-shirt, but you insist on using a cute woven fabric. Sure, you get to say, "Look what I made!" when you finish. But looking is all that's going to happen because you won't be able to get that T-shirt over your head. Unless the garment is really loose fitting, woven fabric needs a fastener, like a zipper or elastic. And who wants to add a zipper to a T-shirt? No one, that's who.

Knit Fabric

What makes knit fabric great? It stretches! It's more comfortable to wear! It doesn't fray! It allows you to create fitted garments without the use of fasteners. Jersey, interlock, sweatshirt, activewear spandex, stretch velvet, and polar fleece are examples of knit fabrics.

Knits are dreamy.

▶ *Sounds like the perfect fabric, right?* Almost. Like all good things, working with knit fabric isn't headache free. It stretches, even when you don't want it to stretch, which can cause all sorts of problems:

Exhibit 1: The reason we might set our knit project on fire

That, my friends, is a wavy neckline. It can happen to your hems, your seams—basically, anywhere you sew. Where there is stretch, there can be stretched out. Knit fabrics have to be handled with extra care to make sure things don't stretch where you don't want them to. This might make some newbies nervous. **But not you, right?** • • • • • • • • • • • • • • • • • • ▶

It's not as scary as it seems, as long as you take your time and take precautions. We'll get through this together and only shed happy tears for a job well done.

Right Side and Wrong Side

Two terms that are common when describing fabric are *right side* and *wrong side*. I'll let Pinny explain this one.

The right side of the fabric is the one who got the answer correct!

▶ *What?* That doesn't make any sense.

The right side of the fabric is the side that looks the nicest, the side you want on the outside of the finished garment. If the fabric has llamas all over it, the side with visible llamas is the right side of the fabric. The opposite side, where the llamas aren't as visible, is the wrong side of the fabric. Or, with satin, the right side has a glossy finish, while the wrong side has a dull finish. There are no strict rules about this. If you prefer the wrong side, then that becomes *your* right side.

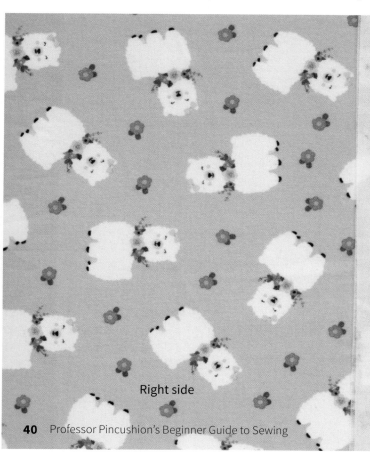

Right side

Wrong side

What if the fabric looks the same on both sides with no print or finish to help you?

Oh-em-gee! Is she wearing that with the wrong side of the fabric showing?

runzelkorn/Shutterstock.com

▶ *Yeah, no one is going to say that because no one will know.*

When it seems impossible to tell the right and wrong side, just pick a side and stick with it. Make a chalk mark on the wrong side of each fabric piece to make a visual clue and maintain consistency through your project. And if someone does point out your "mistake," you can always go with:

Yeah. Obviously.

shurkin_son/Shutterstock.com

Then sashay away with confidence, because you and I both know you look good. Not everyone can see genius. It's sad, really. Ah, well. You keep sashaying with your genius, creative heart.

Chapter Four

Fun with Knit Fabric

PROJECT TIME
T-Shirt Upcycling

Ready to learn some more?

> **More? My brain is tired!**

▶ *It is a lot.* Let's take a break by doing some fun exercises that teach us to work with knit fabric. The garment most associated with knit fabric: the humble T-shirt. ⋯⋯⋯⋯▶

We love to wear them, plus there's also lots of room to take a simple T-shirt and add style to it. Because knit fabric doesn't fray, we can do some really creative and easy things.

> **Old wardrobe pieces can get a new identity.**

▶ *Exactly.* Grab fabric scissors and an old T-shirt, and let's experiment with a few ideas.

Alter the Neckline

First, you can cut off the existing neckband to change the shirt's neckline.

What? Really? Just cut it with scissors? But what if I mess it up?

▶ *The first cut is the scariest,* but that's why you're experimenting on a T-shirt that isn't near and dear to your heart. Jump in with those scissors and start snipping. Here are some ideas:

Cut to create a wider neckline.

Cut out a notch.

Do a patterned cutout. Leave the neckband and cut a shape (or shapes) below it.

If you're extra nervous, use a fabric marker or chalk to draw guidelines directly on the T-shirt before cutting.

Alter the Sleeves

There's also a lot you can do with sleeves.

Cut off the sleeves to create a tank top.

Cut off the top portion of each sleeve to create a cold-shoulder style.

Cut slits along the top of the sleeve to create a fringed style.

Alter the Body of the T-Shirt

Here are some other ideas you can try:

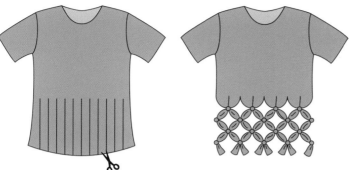

Cut off the bottom and then cut slits to create a crop top with fringe. As a bonus, you can tie fringe strands together to create a macramé effect.

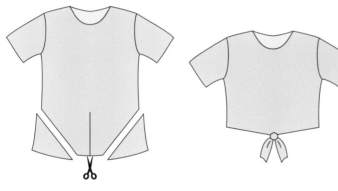

Cut off most of the bottom, but leave a triangle shape at the front center of the shirt. Then cut up the center of the T-shirt at least 5˝. Now tie the two sides into a knot.

Create a shredded design by marking an outline shape and then cutting shreds inside of it.

Those are just a few ideas, but you can really get creative and experiment. Your homework is to take a T-shirt and make it different than it was before. You can try out some of my ideas or come up with some of your own. Take before-and-after pictures to track the transformation. Most of all, let your creativity flow.

Working with T-shirts is easy. What else can we make?

▶ *How about we stick with a T-shirt,* but we add in our sewing machine?

PROJECT TIME
T-Shirt Bag

The T-shirt bag is a great way to recycle an old garment. In this lesson, you'll learn how to:

▶ choose a needle

▶ set stitch length

▶ backstitch

▶ sew two pieces of fabric together

FABRIC

An old T-shirt

NOTIONS

All-purpose thread

TOOLS

Sewing machine

Straight pins

Scissors

Ballpoint sewing machine needle, size 80/12

Preparing the T-Shirt

STEP 1 Cut off the neckline of the T-shirt. This is going to be the bag's main opening.

STEP 2 Cut off both sleeves. The shoulders of the T-shirt will become the handles.

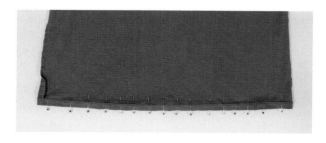

STEP 3 Turn the T-shirt inside out. This means that the "right side" of the T-shirt is on the inside. Lay flat and match the front and back bottom hemlines of the T-shirt, inserting straight pins to hold both layers of fabric together.

Break Time: Needles

But I'm ready to press that foot pedal to the metal.

▶ *Someone's getting brave!* But we can't always jump on the machine and start sewing, especially without ensuring the settings are right.

First, the sewing machine needs the correct needle. When shopping for sewing machine needles, there are a lot of different types and sizes to choose from. To keep things simple, these are the most common needles and their uses:

Fabric Type	Needle Type
Woven	Sharp
Knit	Ballpoint
Unknown	Universal (can work with most fabrics)

Needles are sized with two numbers divided by a slash, like 90/14. The number 90 is the European size and 14 is the American size.

When it comes to needle sizing, the higher the number on the needle, the heavier the fabric it should be used with. For example, denim might need a 100/16 needle, while chiffon would use a 65/9. For the projects in this book, we'll use a needle in the middle: 80/12.

What needle should we use for our T-shirt bag? A ballpoint 80/12. Why? Because it's a midweight knit fabric.

Replace the needle in your machine now. Need a refresher on how to change the needle? Go back to Chapter Two (page 33).

A normal **stitch length** setting for sewing seams is 2.5. You might use a 3 for heavyweight fabric or a 2 for lightweight fabric. For this project, set it to a 2.5.

The **stitch width** setting should be at a 0 for a straight stitch. No zigzagging yet.

For **thread tension**, the standard setting is fine. I have mine at a 4.

Okay, after you've done your sewing piloting precheck, you are ready.

I put in a new needle. Now can we start sewing?

▶ *Almost.* First, let's check the stitch settings.

Starting to Sew

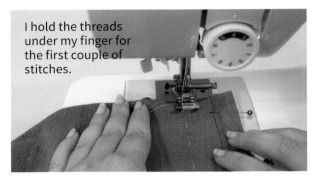

I hold the threads under my finger for the first couple of stitches.

STEP 4 It's time to sew a seam above the stitches of the shirt's original hem. You can sew just above the hem or a couple inches above it, depending on how deep you want your bag to be. If you want to draw a chalk guideline, you can. Lift the presser foot, slide the fabric underneath, and start at one end of the pinned section.

STEP 5 Before pressing the foot pedal, put the thread tails under your left hand to hold them. Otherwise, they sometimes get sucked back into the machine and create a small thready bird's nest on the backside of your project.

Sew a couple stitches and then stop. You don't want your stitches to come out, so when sewing a seam, you need to begin and end with a backstitch. This is the sewing machine's version of tying a knot. Push the stitch reversal (U-turn) button, and press down on the foot pedal. The sewing machine will stitch backward. You only need to do a couple stitches. Then release to sew forward again. This is called backstitching.

STEP 6 Sew the whole length of the pinned area. I like to remove pins as I go instead of sewing over them. Accidentally sewing over them is usually fine, but once in a while, the needle will hit a straight pin, and the needle will break. Then a new needle has to be inserted. Plus, the sound of needles breaking is scary.

Don't run me over!

When sewing, let the machine do the work of pulling the fabric through. No strong-arming. Your job is to lightly guide the fabric in order to make sure the machine sews straight. The machine's job is to feed the fabric through and stitch.

STEP 7 At the end, don't forget to backstitch again for a couple stitches. We don't want to do all this work only to have the bag fall apart, dropping whatever's inside into a dirty puddle.

Cut threads to detach the fabric from the sewing machine.

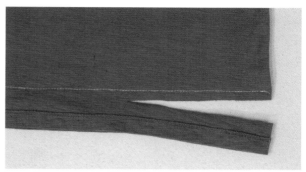

STEP 8 Raise the presser foot and needle, turning the handwheel if necessary, then remove the fabric. Trim the threads.

STEP 9 Use fabric scissors to cut off the original T-shirt hem. This removes bulk. But don't cut too close to the new stitches; leave a little breathing room.

That humble T-shirt is now a humble shopping bag. Perfect for carrying new fabric to add to your stash.

Am I a sewist now?

STEP 10 Flip your new T-shirt bag right side out. It's ready to be used! Go ahead and give it a test carry.

▶ *Great job.* You made something with your sewing machine! But don't stop here; there are more projects ahead of you to continue leveling up your sewing XP.

Chapter Five
Fun with Woven Fabric

Now that we've created an easy project with knit fabric, it's time to get our feet wet with woven fabric. Instead of recycling an old garment, let's create something from scratch. Remember young Professor Pincushion's favorite project? The hair scrunchie!

If you're about to say, "But I don't wear/like/want hair scrunchies." That's okay. Make it for someone else. Or think of it as a fabric projectile for an Ultimate Scrunchie Battle. This is about developing skills, and making a scrunchie is one of the simplest projects for beginners. Trust me, you'll learn a lot, and you might even decide to make more for fun.

This is how you go into battle.

Hair Scrunchie

The scrunchie is a circular tube of fabric with elastic running through it. In this lesson, you'll learn how to:

▶ create a seam allowance

▶ run elastic through a casing

▶ hand sew a running stitch

▶ hand sew a slip stitch

FABRIC

Cotton woven fabric, such as quilter's cotton (at least 5″ × 18″ (12.7 × 45.7cm))

NOTIONS

¼″ (6mm)–wide elastic (at least 8″ (20.3 cm) long)

All-purpose thread

TOOLS

Sewing machine

Straight pins

Hand-sewing needle

Sewing gauge

Fabric scissors

Fabric chalk

Ruler

Small safety pin

Preparing the Fabric

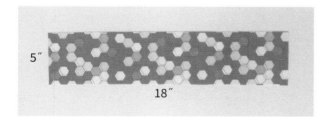

STEP 1 Cut a piece of fabric that's 5″ × 18″ (12.7cm × 45.7cm). To do this, use a straight ruler and fabric chalk to make an outline. Then cut along the outline. Or cut a piece of paper that's this dimension, lay the paper pattern on (or pin it to) your fabric, draw around it, and cut the fabric out.

STEP 2 With the right side of the fabric facing up, fold the fabric in half lengthwise. Instead of it being 5″ (12.7cm) on the short side, it's now 2½″ (6.4cm).

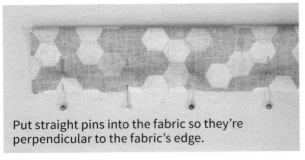

Put straight pins into the fabric so they're perpendicular to the fabric's edge.

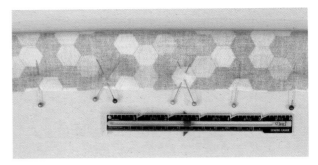

One long side has a fold, while the other long side is where the raw edges meet. Pin the long raw edges together.

Somewhere near the center, use straight pins to form two X's about 2½″ (6.4cm) apart from each other. Use the sewing gauge to measure.

Break Time: Let's Learn About Seams

What are seams and seam allowances?

When two fabric pieces are sewn together, this is called a seam. Inspect your shirt. There are probably seams on the shirt's sides and around the armholes (if there are sleeves).

Garments are full of seams.

▶ **That's right.** It's really hard to make something with one single piece of fabric. Instead, we sew different pieces together. It's like completing a fabric puzzle.

If you think a seam allowance is related to seams, give yourself bonus sewing XP. Remember, woven fabric frays, which can lead to stitches slipping off raw edges. Because of this, we normally don't sew seams directly on the fabric's edge. Instead, we sew a little bit away from the raw edge. The distance between our seam stitches and the raw edge is known as the seam allowance.

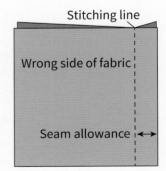

Stitching line

Wrong side of fabric

Seam allowance

If I say to sew a ½″ (1.2cm) seam allowance, that means you should leave ½″ between the stitches and the raw edge.

But how do I do that?

▶ **Great question.** Under the sewing machine's presser foot there's a metal plate with lines. If I say to sew a ⅝″ (1.6cm) seam allowance, then you'd match the fabric's edge with the ⅝″ line. As long as the edge stays there as you sew, there will be a perfect ⅝″ seam allowance. If your machine's lines aren't clearly marked, use the sewing gauge to measure from the sewing needle and place a piece of tape on the sewing machine base for a clear visual guide.

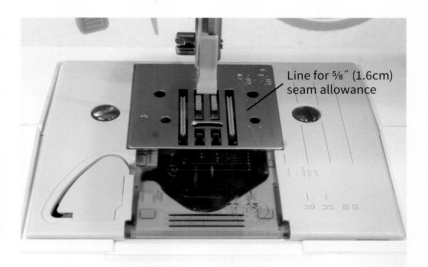

Line for ⅝″ (1.6cm) seam allowance

But why can't you sew stitches wherever you want? Sorry, willy-nilly sewing is not recommended. Projects are created with a specific seam allowance in mind. If I sew all my seams with a 1″ (2.5cm) seam allowance instead of the ⅝″ (1.6cm) seam allowance called for in a pattern, the overall garment will end up smaller. And then I'm crying because it doesn't fit.

I'm a rebel, Professor.

▶ *In sewing, you can either be a rebel or have clothes that fit.* If you still want to be a rebel, be one with your fashion and fabric choices, not with your seam allowances.

Sewing the First Seam

STEP 3 Make sure the sewing machine is threaded correctly. If there's still a ballpoint needle from the knit project, change it to a universal or sharp needle, size 80/12.

On the pinned side of the fabric, sew a ¼″ (6mm) seam allowance. If the machine doesn't have a ¼″ line on the metal plate, use your sewing gauge to measure from the needle. *Do not* sew between the X pins.

▶ *Start sewing at one end, and stop at the first X.* Then move the fabric past the second X and continue sewing to the end.

X marks the spot where you stop.

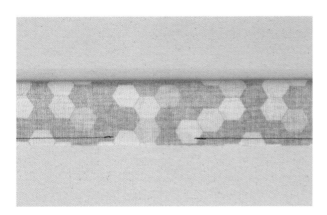

IMPORTANT: Don't forget to push that U-turn button to do a backstitch at the beginning and end of the seam to create a knot on each end.

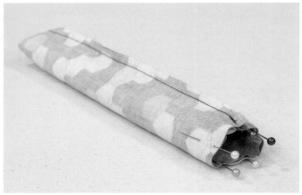

STEP 4 Now you have a tube of fabric with a gap in the center. Take one end of the tube and push it through itself until both ends are together and the raw edges match. The tube will be half the length it just was. Pin the edges, matching the seamlines. For now, ignore the center gap (though it can be used to help move the fabric through the tube).

STEP 5 Next, it's time to sew another ¼″ seam, but the tube is too small to sew on the sewing machine. Ha! And you thought I was kidding about that hand-sewing part.

Break Time: Let's Thread a Hand Needle

Cut a piece of thread about 14″ (35.6cm) long and slip it through the eye of the hand needle, extending past the eye by only about 4″ (10.2cm). The short end is the thread tail. On the other end of the thread, tie a knot by creating a loop, putting the end of the thread through the loop, and pulling. I like to tie it twice to create a bigger knot.

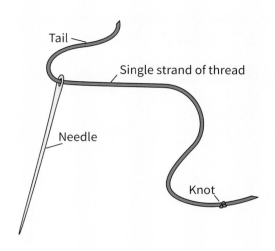

Tail

Single strand of thread

Needle

Knot

Hand Stitching

STEP 6 Use fabric chalk and a sewing gauge to measure and mark the fabric for a guideline around the perimeter of the tube, about ¼″ (6mm) away from the raw edge. Use the threaded needle to sew one of the most basic hand stitches, the *running stitch*.

A running stitch is what the Professor used before the invention of the sewing machine.

▶ *Uh, excuse me.* The sewing machine was invented in 1846. Obviously, Pinny doesn't know how age works. Or Pinny's revealing my Highlander secrets.

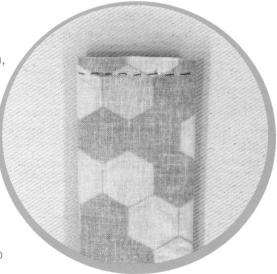

Put the needle through the fabric on the chalk mark from the outside to the inside of the tube. When pulling the needle through, make sure to hold it at the needle eye, pinching so the thread doesn't slip out and force you to rethread. Then move the needle parallel to the edge and pass it back through the fabric from the inside to the outside of the tube. Go in and out, in and out, until the stitches go all the way around the tube. Don't sew the tube shut. The stitches (and the gaps between the stitches) should be small, about ⅛″ (3mm) in length.

At the end, run the needle through a little bit of fabric to create a thread loop and then put the needle through the loop, pulling to create a knot. Cut the thread.

Wow! It's a floppy fabric donut.

STEP 7 Remember that gap between the X pins? Grab the fabric inside the gap and pull it out; you will end up with a circular tube of fabric, right side out.

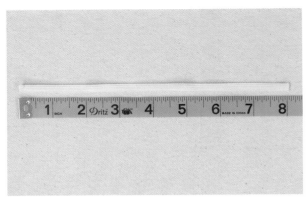

STEP 8 Next, take ¼″ (6mm)–wide elastic and cut a piece that is 8″ (20.3cm) in length.

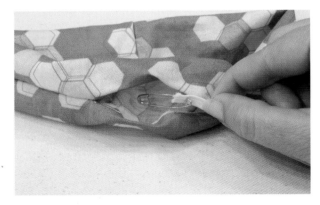

On one end of the elastic, attach a small safety pin. Slip the safety pin end into the gap in the fabric tube. Then, pin the other end of the elastic to the outside of the fabric, near the gap.

The safety pin gives us something substantial to hold on to inside the tube, making it easier to run the elastic through the casing. Hold the safety pin from the outside of the tube with one hand, gather fabric on it, and (while still holding the safety pin) pull the fabric behind it. The elastic will begin to make its way through the tube.

STEP 9 Overlap the two elastic ends by at least a ½″ (1.2cm) and pin.

Switch the sewing machine to the zigzag stitch and increase the stitch width to a 3. Sew a zigzag stitch across the overlapped elastic only (not the fabric), using the stitch reversal button to go over the area a few times to make it extra secure. This might be tricky, but pull your elastic away from the tube to make it easier.

STEP 10 Hey, guess what? This is the last step. Stretch the scrunchie, and the elastic should slip inside the casing. Because the elastic is shorter than the fabric tube, the fabric will bunch and have the typical gathered scrunchie look.

Now to get rid of that pesky gap with a hand *slip stitch*. Thread the hand needle, same as before. Pull on each side of the gap, and the fabric edge will tuck itself inside the scrunchie. Pin this area until the gap is closed.

A slip stitch sews folded edge to folded edge. The first stitch should start near the raw edge inside the scrunchie in order to hide the knot. Put the needle through the fabric on one folded side. Then pull the needle through the folded edge on the opposite side. Go back to the first folded edge and repeat until the gap is sewn closed. Tie a knot.

That's it!
You just made a hair scrunchie.

If you're saying to yourself,
"Wow, that took forever," don't
worry. That's because it was your first
one. Now that you've gone through the process, your next one can be
done faster. But we're not stopping here. We have so much more to learn.

Chapter Six
Intro to Patterns

You must be feeling pretty confident at this point. You've conquered your fear of the sewing machine, you can recycle T-shirts like nobody's business, and you have matching hair scrunchies for every outfit.

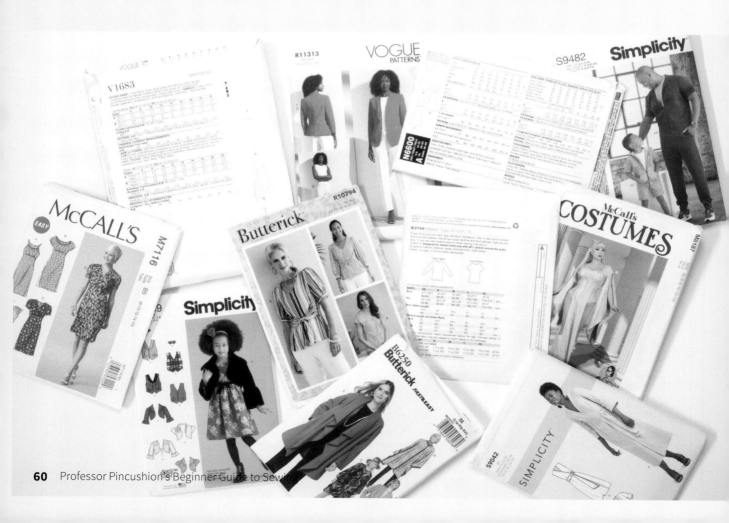

There's nothing we can't sew.

▶ *You shouldn't take on a ten-piece Renaissance costume just yet,* but you're leveling up nicely. It's time to take on a greater challenge: using commercial patterns. People have been using patterns to sew clothes for a long time regardless of their skill level.

In the old days, not only did a candy bar cost a nickel, but a pattern was 50¢. Sweet bargains.

Image courtesy of SIMPLICITY® by Design Group Americas

Image courtesy of SIMPLICITY® by Design Group Americas

Commercial patterns are training wheels for beginners. They provide paper pattern pieces plus step-by-step directions so sewists will know exactly how to cut out fabric pieces and assemble them into a specific garment or project. Who doesn't like a helpful boost?

Maybe you've feasted your eyes on something like this and thought, "Yes, that's exactly what I want to make."

Unfortunately, while commercial patterns make things easier, they aren't immediately easy to use. Learning how to read and understand commercial patterns is a skill. Jumping in can be overwhelming. Pinny doesn't like this because tears make him rusty. So, let's break everything down.

The next best thing to a fabric stash is a pattern stash.

Lookbooks

The most common places to purchase commercial patterns are online or in a fabric store. Perusing patterns in a fabric store is fun and puts you in close proximity to all the fabric. But if going to a store is not convenient, I have good news. Patterns can also be purchased from pattern company websites, many of which offer downloadable versions to print and assemble at home. It might be time to get your printer in shape and finally address the "low cyan ink" indicator that keeps blinking.

In a fabric store, there will be a table or cabinets with several large catalogs. I like to call these catalogs "dream books" because they help me dream about all the amazing clothes I can make. But the real name for them is **lookbooks**.

Flip through lookbook pages really quickly and it'll look like the models are walking on a fashion runway. (Just kidding. But that would be fun, right?)

Image courtesy of McCall's® by Design Group Americas

Lookbooks are a way to search for patterns available in print. The books are separated into categories like formalwear, costumes, and others.

To start, ask yourself the question:

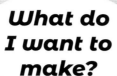

What do I want to make?

▶ *If you know exactly what you want to make, you can flip to a specific section.* Or if you prefer the dream approach, you can scan through the whole book. If you don't find the perfect garment in the first book, search through another one. Most fabric stores carry multiple lines of patterns. As a beginner, start off with patterns marked as *easy*. Sure, this limits your choices, but it's not a good idea to start with the hard stuff. Even the easy patterns will provide a challenge. Here's an example of a lookbook page:

The first thing that draws your attention is the picture ❶. Maybe it's something that makes you ooh and ahh. Sometimes you'll get only one design, and sometimes you'll get multiple garments or variations ❷. Lucky you!

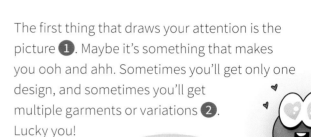

Yup, this is the pattern for me.

Next, it's time to locate the pattern in one of the store's pattern cabinets. You'll need the pattern brand ❸ and the specific numerical ID ❹. With these two things, head to the brand-labeled cabinet, and then use the ID to find the pattern inside. Be careful not to grab and go. You need the pattern envelope that includes your size. One envelope may not include all sizes, but a specific range.

Image courtesy of McCall's® by Design Group Americas

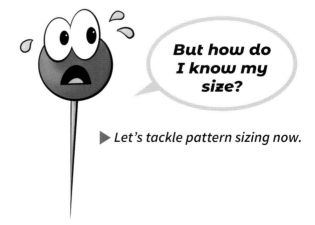

But how do I know my size?

▶ *Let's tackle pattern sizing now.*

Choosing a Pattern Size

Retail sizing and pattern sizing are not the same, meaning that even if you wear a size 4 dress from your favorite store, you won't necessarily use a size 4 pattern. Pattern companies have their own system, and this system is consistent. A size 12 in one pattern line is usually a size 12 in most of them. This is actually easier than retail clothing because each individual retail brand may decide for itself what sizing scale to use.

Grab a flexible tape measure to figure out your pattern size before going to the fabric store.

Ask a friend for help. But don't lasso them with the tape measure.

SIZE
PERFECT

The only garment tag you need

When taking body measurements, wear fitted clothes (nothing bulky). It's best to have a friend help so that you can stand straight and not slouch, which could affect your measurements. Remember my big sewing secret?

▶ **Measure accurately.** The only people who will know your numbers are you and your bestest, most wonderful measuring friend. (Or choose someone with very poor recall skills.) The most amazing part? You can sew in your own sizing tag!

Using a Ruler

Time to learn fractions. Because measuring accurately is important, there's no rounding. Let me repeat this: We don't round to the nearest inch because it's easier. Think of it like a snowball. One little fudge might be okay, but then this snowball starts rolling downhill, building on more inaccuracies, and before you know it …

Pow! Poorly fitting clothes.

Well, that escalated quickly.

We only need to break down one inch to understand the whole ruler. From the end of the tape measure to the number 1 is 1 inch (1″). But what about all those tiny lines in between? Each of those lines mark a fraction of an inch, and there are eight lines, including the inch line. So, each line is 1 out of 8, or, one-eighth of an inch (⅛″). If I say to count five of those tiny lines, then that's 5 out of 8, or five-eighths of an inch (⅝″). Easy, right? What is it if I say four lines?

⁴/₈″

▶ *I like the enthusiasm.* That is the correct answer … kind of. Four lines is the halfway mark, right? Because it's smack in the middle of an inch, it's a half-inch (½″). Take that half-inch, cut it in half again, and it would be ²⁄₈, or a quarter of an inch (¼″). The measurement ⁶⁄₈ is three-quarters of an inch (¾″). So, if I say a measurement is 3¾″, that means it would be three inch lines plus six little lines. Here's a complete inch breakdown.

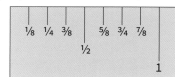

Measuring Your Body

Let's take a look at a pattern body-measurement chart example to figure out sizing.

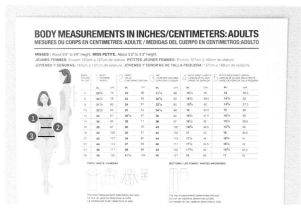

These can be found in lookbooks, on pattern envelopes, and on pattern websites.

On a standard sizing chart, sizes are separated into categories of *children*, *misses*, *women*, and *men*. What you want to make will determine which body measurements are needed. For a pair of *misses'* pants, the most important measurement would be the hipline (line ❸ on the model). Why? Because this is usually the widest part of the

body on this particular garment, so it's the most important one to match. For men's pants, the waistline tends to be more important. For either of these garments, the bust or chest measurement (line ❶ on the model) is not needed because it's not relevant to pants.

This chart comes in handy because we don't always fit into a nice and easy, standard pattern size. Don't be surprised if you wear a size 20 for pants, but a size 16 for a top.

To take a body measurement—for example, the hipline—wrap the tape measure, starting with the zero end, around the body at the widest part of the hip. The tape measure should be level with the floor. It shouldn't be very tight or loose, just comfortable. Read the measurement and write it down. Repeat this with the waistline, bustline, chest, and any others. Match these measurements to the chart to find a pattern size. If you're between sizes, opt for the larger pattern because it can always be altered to fit.

Gathering Supplies

Once you know your size, choose the correct pattern. This envelope contains sizes 6–14.

The front of the pattern envelope looks pretty, but flip it over to the back to find all the juicy information: What type of fabric should you use? How much fabric do you need? What notions are required?

Let's take a look at an example:

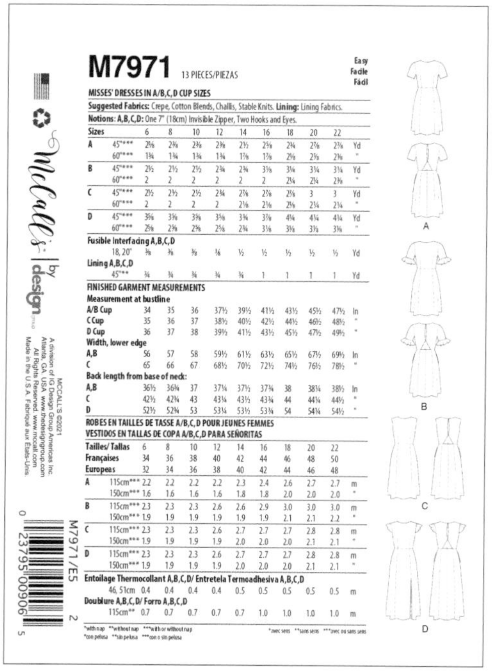

M7971 13 PIECES/PIEZAS — Easy / Facile / Fácil

MISSES' DRESSES IN A/B,C,D CUP SIZES

Suggested Fabrics: Crepe, Cotton Blends, Challis, Stable Knits. **Lining:** Lining Fabrics.

Notions: A,B,C,D: One 7" (18cm) Invisible Zipper, Two Hooks and Eyes.

Sizes		6	8	10	12	14	16	18	20	22	
A	45"***	2⅜	2⅜	2⅜	2⅜	2½	2⅝	2¾	2⅞	2⅞	Yd
	60"***	1¾	1¾	1¾	1¾	1⅞	1⅞	2⅛	2⅛	2⅛	"
B	45"***	2½	2½	2½	2¾	2¾	3⅛	3¼	3¼	3¼	Yd
	60"***	2	2	2	2	2	2	2¼	2¼	2⅜	"
C	45"***	2½	2½	2½	2¾	2⅞	2⅞	2⅞	3	3	Yd
	60"***	2	2	2	2	2⅛	2⅛	2⅛	2¼	2¼	"
D	45"***	3⅝	3⅝	3⅝	3⅝	3¾	3⅞	4¼	4¼	4¼	Yd
	60"***	2⅝	2⅝	2⅝	2⅝	2¾	3⅛	3⅛	3⅛	3⅛	"
Fusible Interfacing A,B,C,D											
	18, 20"	⅜	⅜	⅜	⅜	½	½	½	½	½	Yd
Lining A,B,C,D											
	45"**	¾	¾	¾	¾	¾	1	1	1	1	Yd
FINISHED GARMENT MEASUREMENTS											
Measurement at bustline											
A/B Cup		34	35	36	37½	39½	41½	43½	45½	47½	In
C Cup		35	36	37	38½	40½	42½	44½	46½	48½	"
D Cup		36	37	38	39½	41½	43½	45½	47½	49½	"
Width, lower edge											
A,B		56	57	58	59½	61½	63½	65½	67½	69½	In
C		65	66	67	68½	70½	72½	74½	76½	78½	"
Back length from base of neck:											
A,B		36½	36¾	37	37¼	37½	37¾	38	38¼	38½	In
C		42½	42¾	43	43¼	43½	43¾	44	44¼	44½	"
D		52½	52¾	53	53¼	53½	53¾	54	54¼	54½	"

ROBES EN TAILLES DE TASSE A/B,C,D POUR JEUNES FEMMES
VESTIDOS EN TALLAS DE COPA A/B,C,D PARA SEÑORITAS

Tailles/ Tallas		6	8	10	12	14	16	18	20	22	
Françaises		34	36	38	40	42	44	46	48	50	
Europeas		32	34	36	38	40	42	44	46	48	
A	115cm***	2.2	2.2	2.2	2.2	2.3	2.4	2.6	2.7	2.7	m
	150cm***	1.6	1.6	1.6	1.6	1.8	1.8	2.0	2.0	2.0	"
B	115cm***	2.3	2.3	2.3	2.6	2.6	2.9	3.0	3.0	3.0	m
	150cm***	1.9	1.9	1.9	1.9	1.9	1.9	2.1	2.1	2.2	"
C	115cm***	2.3	2.3	2.3	2.6	2.7	2.7	2.7	2.8	2.8	m
	150cm***	1.9	1.9	1.9	1.9	2.0	2.0	2.0	2.1	2.1	"
D	115cm***	2.3	2.3	2.3	2.6	2.7	2.7	2.7	2.8	2.8	m
	150cm***	1.9	1.9	1.9	1.9	2.0	2.0	2.0	2.1	2.1	"
Entoilage Thermocollant A,B,C,D/ Entretela Termoadhesiva A,B,C,D											
	46, 51cm	0.4	0.4	0.4	0.4	0.5	0.5	0.5	0.5	0.5	m
Doublure A,B,C,D/ Forro A,B,C,D											
	115cm**	0.7	0.7	0.7	0.7	0.7	1.0	1.0	1.0	1.0	m

*with nap **without nap ***with or without nap
*con pelusa **sin pelusa ***con o sin pelusa
*avec sens **sans sens ***avec ou sans sens

MCCALL'S ©2021

M7971/E5

Image courtesy of McCall's by Design Group Americas

McCall's
M7971
Sizes
(6-8-10-12-14)
B
C
A
D
#JunieMcCalls
This sewing pattern includes multiple view options with simple instructions. Show your make! Use the hashtag provided.
Ce patron de couture comprend plusieurs modèles avec des instructions faciles! Montrez votre réalisation! Utilisez le hashtag fourni.
Este patrón de costura incluye varios modelos con instrucciones fáciles! Muestre su confección! Use el hashtag proporcionado.

Image courtesy of McCall's by Design Group Americas

Yikes! That's too many words.

It's tempting to turn it back to the pretty picture side—but wait! Let's take a breath and power through. First of all, if some of it reads like a foreign language . . . well, that's because it is. The same information appears in multiple languages. If you only need English, you can ignore half of it. See? It's already getting less overwhelming.

The back of the pattern is separated into nice, manageable bite-size pieces. Yum.

Let's do it!

M7971 13 PIECES/PIEZAS

Easy
Facile
Fácil

MISSES' DRESSES IN A/B,C,D CUP SIZES

Suggested Fabrics: Crepe, Cotton Blends, Challis, Stable Knits. **Lining:** Lining Fabrics. ❷

Notions: A,B,C,D: One 7" (18cm) Invisible Zipper, Two Hooks and Eyes. ❸

❹

Sizes		6	8	10	12	14	16	18	20	22	
A	45"***	2⅜	2⅜	2⅜	2⅜	2½	2⅝	2¾	2⅞	2⅞	Yd
	60"***	1¾	1¾	1¾	1¾	1⅞	1⅞	2⅛	2⅛	2⅛	"
B	45"***	2½	2½	2½	2¾	2¾	3⅛	3¼	3¼	3¼	Yd
	60"***	2	2	2	2	2	2	2¼	2¼	2⅜	"
C	45"***	2½	2½	2½	2¾	2⅞	2⅞	2⅞	3	3	Yd
	60"***	2	2	2	2	2⅛	2⅛	2⅛	2¼	2¼	"
D	45"***	3⅝	3⅝	3⅝	3⅝	3¾	3⅞	4¼	4¼	4¼	Yd
	60"***	2⅝	2⅝	2⅝	2⅝	2¾	3⅛	3⅛	3⅛	3⅛	"
Fusible Interfacing A,B,C,D											
	18, 20"	⅜	⅜	⅜	⅜	½	½	½	½	½	Yd
Lining A,B,C,D											
	45"**	¾	¾	¾	¾	¾	1	1	1	1	Yd

❺

FINISHED GARMENT MEASUREMENTS										
Measurement at bustline										
A/B Cup	34	35	36	37½	39½	41½	43½	45½	47½	In
C Cup	35	36	37	38½	40½	42½	44½	46½	48½	"
D Cup	36	37	38	39½	41½	43½	45½	47½	49½	"
Width, lower edge										
A,B	56	57	58	59½	61½	63½	65½	67½	69½	In
C	65	66	67	68½	70½	72½	74½	76½	78½	"
Back length from base of neck:										
A,B	36½	36¾	37	37¼	37½	37¾	38	38¼	38½	In
C	42½	42¾	43	43¼	43½	43¾	44	44¼	44½	"
D	52½	52¾	53	53¼	53½	53¾	54	54¼	54½	"

ROBES EN TAILLES DE TASSE A/B,C,D POUR JEUNES FEMMES
VESTIDOS EN TALLAS DE COPA A/B,C,D PARA SEÑORITAS

Tailles/ Tallas		6	8	10	12	14	16	18	20	22	
Françaises		34	36	38	40	42	44	46	48	50	
Europeas		32	34	36	38	40	42	44	46	48	
A	115cm***	2.2	2.2	2.2	2.2	2.3	2.4	2.6	2.7	2.7	m
	150cm***	1.6	1.6	1.6	1.6	1.8	1.8	2.0	2.0	2.0	"
B	115cm***	2.3	2.3	2.3	2.6	2.6	2.9	3.0	3.0	3.0	m
	150cm***	1.9	1.9	1.9	1.9	1.9	1.9	2.1	2.1	2.2	"
C	115cm***	2.3	2.3	2.3	2.6	2.7	2.7	2.7	2.8	2.8	m
	150cm***	1.9	1.9	1.9	1.9	2.0	2.0	2.0	2.1	2.1	"
D	115cm***	2.3	2.3	2.3	2.6	2.7	2.7	2.7	2.8	2.8	m
	150cm***	1.9	1.9	1.9	1.9	2.0	2.0	2.0	2.1	2.1	"
Entoilage Thermocollant A,B,C,D/ Entretela Termoadhesiva A,B,C,D											
	46, 51cm	0.4	0.4	0.4	0.4	0.5	0.5	0.5	0.5	0.5	m
Doublure A,B,C,D/ Forro A,B,C,D											
	115cm**	0.7	0.7	0.7	0.7	0.7	1.0	1.0	1.0	1.0	m

*with nap **without nap ***with or without nap
*con pelusa **sin pelusa ***con o sin pelusa

*avec sens **sans sens ***avec ou sans sens

❶

McCall's | by design group

M7971/E5 2

0 23795 00906 5

Image courtesy of McCall's by Design Group Americas

❶ These are the different design views (options) available inside the envelope. You'll notice they match up with the pretty pictures on the front of the envelope. In this example, you would pick if you want to make Dress A, B, C, or D.

❷ This is the fabric recommendation section. Isn't that nice of them? It's like they're giving all the answers to a test and it's not even considered cheating. This doesn't mean these are the *only* fabrics that can be used, but it points you in the right direction. If all the fabrics listed are woven fabrics, choosing knit isn't a good idea. Also, in this example, the dress has a lining, so they recommend a main fabric and a lining fabric.

❸ Next are notions. For this dress, you'll need thread, a 7″ (18cm) zipper, and two hook and eyes (a type of fastener). These notions are needed for all design views. If the notions were only needed for view A, the letter A would be next to the information.

Continued on next page

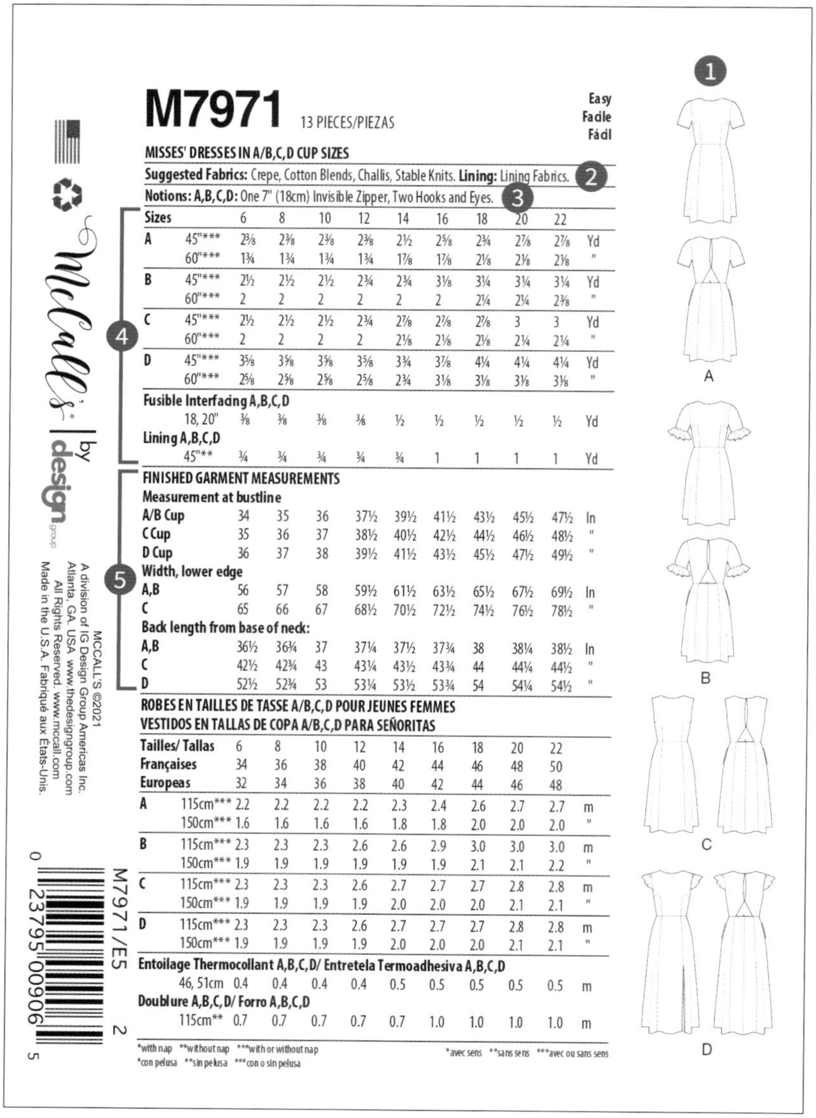

M7971

13 PIECES/PIEZAS

Easy
Facile
Fácil

MISSES' DRESSES IN A/B,C,D CUP SIZES

Suggested Fabrics: Crepe, Cotton Blends, Challis, Stable Knits. **Lining:** Lining Fabrics. (2)

Notions: A,B,C,D: One 7" (18cm) Invisible Zipper, Two Hooks and Eyes. (3)

(4)

Sizes		6	8	10	12	14	16	18	20	22	
A	45"***	2⅜	2⅜	2⅜	2⅜	2½	2⅝	2¾	2⅞	2⅞	Yd
	60"***	1¾	1¾	1¾	1¾	1⅞	1⅞	2⅛	2⅛	2⅛	"
B	45"***	2½	2½	2½	2¾	2¾	3⅛	3¼	3¼	3¼	Yd
	60"***	2	2	2	2	2	2	2¼	2¼	2⅜	"
C	45"***	2½	2½	2½	2¾	2⅞	2⅞	2⅞	3	3	Yd
	60"***	2	2	2	2	2⅛	2⅛	2⅛	2¼	2¼	"
D	45"***	3⅝	3⅝	3⅝	3⅝	3¾	3⅞	4¼	4¼	4¼	Yd
	60"***	2⅝	2⅝	2⅝	2⅝	2¾	3⅛	3⅛	3⅛	3⅛	"
Fusible Interfacing A,B,C,D											
	18, 20"	⅜	⅜	⅜	⅜	½	½	½	½	½	Yd
Lining A,B,C,D											
	45"**	¾	¾	¾	¾	¾	1	1	1	1	Yd

(5)

FINISHED GARMENT MEASUREMENTS	6	8	10	12	14	16	18	20	22	
Measurement at bustline										
A/B Cup	34	35	36	37½	39½	41½	43½	45½	47½	In
C Cup	35	36	37	38½	40½	42½	44½	46½	48½	"
D Cup	36	37	38	39½	41½	43½	45½	47½	49½	"
Width, lower edge										
A,B	56	57	58	59½	61½	63½	65½	67½	69½	In
C	65	66	67	68½	70½	72½	74½	76½	78½	"
Back length from base of neck:										
A,B	36½	36¾	37	37¼	37½	37¾	38	38¼	38½	In
C	42½	42¾	43	43¼	43½	43¾	44	44¼	44½	"
D	52½	52¾	53	53¼	53½	53¾	54	54¼	54½	"

ROBES EN TAILLES DE TASSE A/B,C,D POUR JEUNES FEMMES
VESTIDOS EN TALLAS DE COPA A/B,C,D PARA SEÑORITAS

Tailles/ Tallas		6	8	10	12	14	16	18	20	22	
Françaises		34	36	38	40	42	44	46	48	50	
Europeas		32	34	36	38	40	42	44	46	48	
A	115cm***	2.2	2.2	2.2	2.2	2.3	2.4	2.6	2.7	2.7	m
	150cm***	1.6	1.6	1.6	1.6	1.8	1.8	2.0	2.0	2.0	"
B	115cm***	2.3	2.3	2.3	2.6	2.6	2.9	3.0	3.0	3.0	m
	150cm***	1.9	1.9	1.9	1.9	1.9	1.9	2.1	2.1	2.2	"
C	115cm***	2.3	2.3	2.3	2.6	2.7	2.7	2.7	2.8	2.8	m
	150cm***	1.9	1.9	1.9	1.9	2.0	2.0	2.0	2.1	2.1	"
D	115cm***	2.3	2.3	2.3	2.6	2.7	2.7	2.7	2.8	2.8	m
	150cm***	1.9	1.9	1.9	1.9	2.0	2.0	2.0	2.1	2.1	"
Entoilage Thermocollant A,B,C,D/ Entretela Termoadhesiva A,B,C,D											
	46, 51cm	0.4	0.4	0.4	0.4	0.5	0.5	0.5	0.5	0.5	m
Doublure A,B,C,D/ Forro A,B,C,D											
	115cm**	0.7	0.7	0.7	0.7	0.7	1.0	1.0	1.0	1.0	m

*with nap **without nap ***with or without nap
*con pelusa **sin pelusa ***con o sin pelusa
*avec sens **sans sens ***avec ou sans sens

(1)
A
B
C
D
McCall's by design group
MCCALL'S ©2021
A division of IG Design Group Americas Inc.
Atlanta, GA. USA www.thedesigngroup.com
All Rights Reserved. www.mccall.com
Made in the U.S.A. Fabriqué aux États-Unis.
M7971/E5 2

Image courtesy of McCall's by Design Group Americas

(4) This section covers fabric amounts needed. Find the box with your design view. They could be listed together or separately. In this example, they are listed separately. There's also 45″ (115cm) and 60″(150cm), followed by yardage amounts. The 45″ and 60″ distinction refers to the fabric width. Fabric usually comes in either 45″ or 60″ width, although odd amounts like 44″ or 58″ also exist. Use the 45″ guide for 44″ and the 60″ guide for 58″ fabrics.

But how do I know how wide my fabric is?!

▶ **Fabric bolts will have a tag on the end of the cardboard** (or online, under the specifications) that lists valuable information like the fabric type, care, price per yard, and width.

To find out how much fabric is recommended, you need to match the pattern size, the design view, and the fabric width on the chart. For example, a size 22 in Dress A with fabric width of 60″ (150cm) requires 2⅛ yards (2m) of fabric. Fabric is cut by the yard or fraction of a yard (or meter outside the United States). Take the chosen fabric to the cutting table (not the register) and ask for a specific amount. Anything that's sold by custom measurements, including lining, interfacing, trims, ribbon, and elastic, will be cut by the store's cutters. If you're still confused on how much fabric to get, ask for help.

This envelope also lists a lining for Dress A and fusible interfacing, which means it suggests extra fabric for the lining. To find out how much you need, check your size on the chart. Interfacing is a stabilizing woven or nonwoven fabric used to stiffen fabric for collars or necklines. Don't skip recommended interfacing because it helps give shape to specific areas of a garment.

5 This is the finished garment measurement chart. As a beginner, I wouldn't stress out too much about this section. It lists the final measurements of the garment, giving you a hint about how the garment will fit when finished. Finished measurements may be larger than those listed under the body measurement size chart. This is because most garments aren't meant to be skin tight. Extra inches (called *ease*) are built in so it's *easier* to move around in the garment. You would still refer to the pattern sizing chart to figure out which size to use.

That's it. We just tackled the pattern envelope. Phew! Your first few times inside a fabric store will probably feel overwhelming, and you may need to ask a store employee for help on where to find things. But don't worry. Pretty soon you'll be an old pro.

Chapter Seven

Working with Patterns

Now that you're familiar with the pattern envelope, let's take a peek inside.

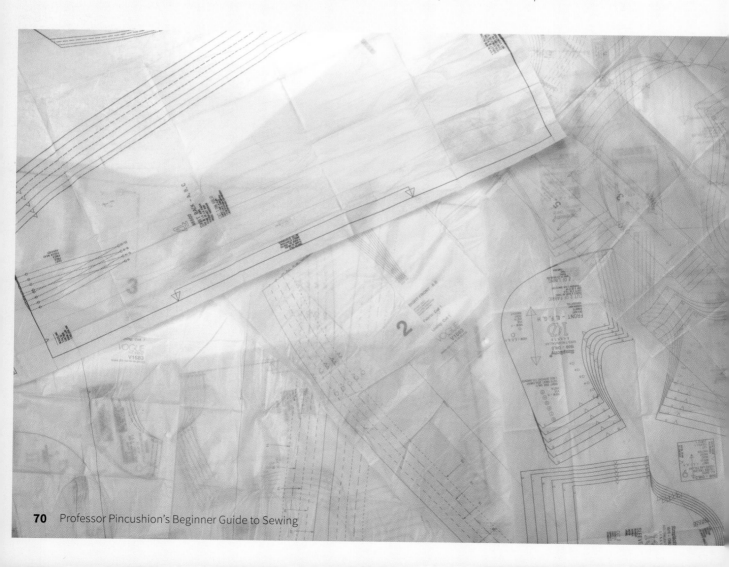

After you open the envelope, don't expect the patterns and envelope to ever be this flat again. Once you take everything out, it blows up to twice the volume. This is the first law of sewing physics.

It takes magic to get patterns back in the envelope neatly.

Inside the envelope are directions and pattern pieces printed on tissue paper. For now, set aside the tissue paper and open the direction pages. Are your eyeballs feeling overwhelmed again? Like everything else with sewing, it's never as scary as you think.

On the first page are the design views **1**. Below this is a pattern piece section **2**. These oddly shaped images are the pattern pieces, and each one is numbered. Listed below is the number and name for each piece, such as *12, Sleeve A B*.

The actual printed tissue paper pattern pieces and the puzzle piece drawings in this section have matching numbers and names. Sewing is easy when everything is consistent and organized.

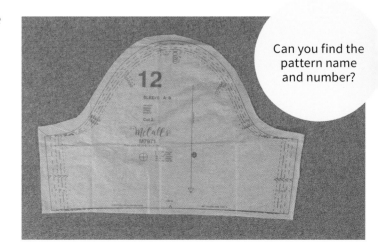

Can you find the pattern name and number?

Cutting Out Pattern Pieces

You only have to cut out the pattern pieces associated with your design view. If there's a letter included, then that particular pattern piece is only needed for that specific design view. For example, *12, Sleeve A B* means that piece *12, Sleeve* is only for Dress A and Dress B. If there's no letter listed, then the pattern piece is for all views. The design view letter is printed on the tissue paper as well. These pattern companies are so helpful!

On the directions, circle or highlight all the pattern pieces you'll need to cut out, like this: • • • • • • • • •▶

Remove the tissue paper and unfold it to find your pattern pieces.

DRESS A, B, C, D
1 BODICE FRONT (A/B Cup)
2 BODICE FRONT (C Cup)
3 BODICE FRONT (D Cup)
4 BODICE BACK
5 ARMHOLE RUFFLE D
6 SKIRT SIDE FRONT
7 SKIRT FRONT
8 SKIRT SIDE BACK
9 SKIRT BACK
10 POCKET
11 SKIRT FACING
12 SLEEVE A B
13 SLEEVE RUFFLE B

VESTIDO A, B, C, D
1 FRENTE DEL CORPIÑO (Copa A/B)
2 FRENTE DEL CORPIÑO (Copa C)
3 FRENTE DEL CORPIÑO (Copa D)
4 ESPALDA DEL CORPIÑO
5 VOLANTE DE LA SISA D
6 COSTADO DEL FRENTE DE LA FALDA
7 FRENTE DE LA FALDA
8 COSTADO DE LA ESPALDA DE LA FALDA
9 ESPALDA DE LA FALDA
10 BOLSILLO
11 VISTA DE LA FALDA
12 MANGA A B
13 VOLANTE DE LA MANGA B

Time to send out the search party, pardner.

▶ **Sometimes more than one pattern piece will have the same number.** This is not a mistake. It's because they've separated the sizes. There might be a pattern piece 10 for size 16 and a pattern piece 10 for size 20. You only cut the one for your size.

Many times, instead of having duplicate pieces for each size, the sizes for one piece will be staggered on top of each other. Here's an example: • • • • • • • • • • • • • • •▶

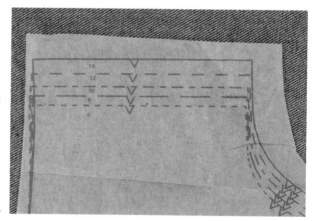

There are several lines, numbered for each size. In this example, there are lines numbered 6, 8, 10, 12, and 14. Those are the sizes. For a size 8, cut on the number 8 line. Many pattern companies make it easy to follow by giving each size line a distinct look by using dashes.

What's the moral of the story today?

Cutting patterns is as easy as cutting on a line. No artistic skills needed here.

▶ *Exactly.* Take your time and make sure to cut the right pattern pieces in the right size. If you're doing that, then you're already conquering this whole sewing-with-a-pattern thing.

TIP

Either cut directly on the line or (my personal preference) cut right outside the line. I like to still see the line when I'm finished.

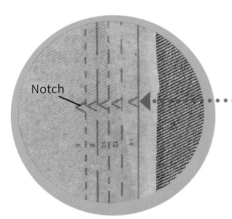

Notch

Oh no! But what's this? Does my pattern have vampire teeth?

▶ *Brave pattern explorers, you have discovered a valuable item: the notch.* Notches help match pieces. They can be single, double, or even triple notches. Whenever you see a notch, give it extra care when cutting.

Just like belly buttons, notches can appear as outies or innies. Cut them either way, as long as they stand out.

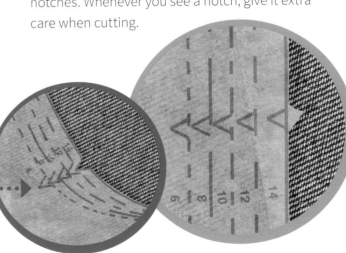

Downloadable Patterns

What if you're using a downloadable pattern? Most of us only have access to standard consumer printers, so pattern companies break up their full-size patterns to fit on standard-size printer paper.

Check the printer settings to ensure the pattern prints at 100% scale, otherwise the pattern pieces might not print at the proper dimensions. If printing from a browser, scale might be found under "more settings." There will be scale lines on one of the printed pages that look like this: •••

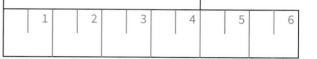

Print only the page with the scale lines and verify they are the exact size as stated. Then print remaining pages.

4″ SCALE SQUARE

1	2	3	4	5	6

Grab some clear tape and follow the directions to tape the corresponding pages together. Sometimes the pages will be numbered in the order they should be laid out, or, like ours, they'll have letters to match to a layout graphic. ••••••▶

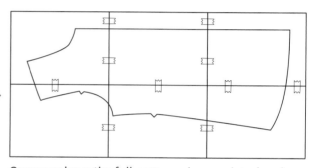

You now have enough information to cut out the downloadable pattern pieces for the shorts pattern included with this book.

Once you have the full pattern pieces printed and put together, you can cut them out in your correct pattern size and use them exactly the same as tissue pattern pieces.

Scan this QR code or visit tinyurl.com/11504-pattern2-download to download the pattern. Do not print from your phone.

Stop! What's that in your hands?

▶ *Did you grab the fabric scissors to cut out your pattern pieces?* For shame. Don't make Pinny and me come over there. But if you grabbed the paper scissors, congrats on making good choices today. Proceed, intrepid newbies.

Treating Our Fabric Right

Let's take a break for a very important topic:
FABRIC.

Should I wash my fabric ahead of time?

▶ *Pinny's asking the right question.* This is called pretreating your fabric. Fabric doesn't come preshrunk. You could make something, wash it, and find that it shrank. Eek!

Wash and dry fabric before cutting any fabric pieces.

Don't learn this lesson the hard way. When shopping, it's important to look at the fabric information tag for care instructions. Not all fabrics are washable, so be careful and choose wisely. You don't want to worry about dry cleaning pajamas because of the fabric you used.

Clothes too small?
Should have pretreated that fabric.

Smokovski/Shutterstock.com

Putting Pattern Pieces to Fabric

The paper pattern pieces are cut. Now what? Time to cut the fabric pieces. Take a look at the instructions; pattern companies are providing all the answers again, this time with a pattern layout.

The pattern layout is the recommended placement of each piece in order to get all the pattern pieces to fit on the fabric. Sometimes there are several layouts, so you need to find the one specific to your project. Find the box that has your design view, fabric width, and pattern size. Match all of those, and you've found your winner.

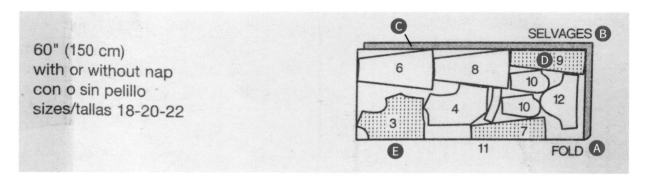

In this example, the piece layout is for 60˝ (150cm) width fabric and sizes 18, 20, and 22.

Fold (A) means the fabric is folded in half. When a pattern piece is cut out of folded fabric, you will get two fabric pieces that are mirror images of each other. For example, if I cut 12 Sleeve, I end up with a right sleeve and a left sleeve.

Selvage (B) indicates the manufactured edge of the fabric (not the cut edge.) If selvage is listed on the top and bottom (instead of fold on one side), that means it's recommended that pattern pieces are pinned to a single layer of fabric. Other times, the pattern might recommend the fabric be partially folded instead of folded perfectly in half.

Some of the illustrated fabric is shaded. This indicates the **right side of the fabric** (C), meaning the fabric is folded in half with the fabric's right side on the inside. Does this mean patterns can't be pinned to the fabric's right side? No, but typically it's done the way shown in the layout, and pieces are pinned on the wrong side of the fabric.

The layout will also indicate which side of a pattern piece should be facing up. Typically, pieces are placed on the fabric right side up, meaning printed side up, but there will be times when they recommend placing the pattern wrong side up. **Wrong-side-up pattern pieces** are polka dotted (D).

Do some pieces look like they're placed on the **fold of the fabric** in the layout (E)? They probably are. On the paper pattern piece, there is an edge indicating that it should be placed on the fabric fold. Instead of getting two fabric pieces after cutting, you get one fabric piece that's twice the size of the pattern.

Why can't I put the patterns however I want?

▶ *You mean … do things willy-nilly?*

You can't see my face right now but, be assured, my right eye is twitching.

The pattern layout is not simply trying to get all the pieces to fit.

It's also considering pattern layout rule number one: grainline, a.k.a. making sure the fabric's fibers lie in the same direction when you put the garment together. Imagine you're using striped fabric. If pattern pieces are placed haphazardly, the final garment could have stripes going every which way.

You're making me dizzy.

▶ ***The grainline is not always visibly obvious,*** but all fabrics have one and, like with striped fabric, it needs to match throughout the whole garment so the fabric will lie correctly on the body. On each pattern piece, there's a line or arrow with the word **grainline**. In a correct layout, this line will be parallel to the selvage, like this:

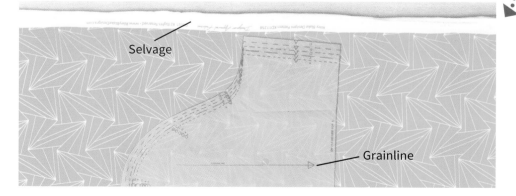

Selvage

Grainline

When placing patterns on fabric, all grainlines should be in the same direction, which will happen if the pattern layout is used. If the grainline rule is followed, you don't *need* the pattern layout, but they're giving it to you. Why not use it?

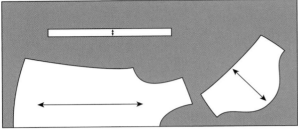

Incorrect grainline placement

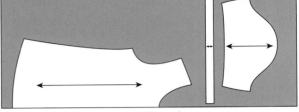

Correct grainline placement

Once pattern pieces are laid out, it's time to use our friend, Pinny, and pin them in place. I recommend putting the straight pin through the pattern and all fabric layers, so it's parallel to the edge of the pattern.

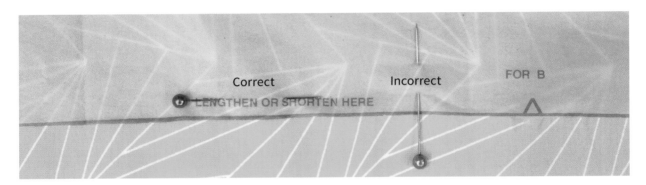

When pinning is done the correct way, the straight pin covers more surface area, and less pins are needed.

Plus, if the straight pin sticks out past the pattern piece (as in the incorrect example), it makes it harder to cut. We don't want to cut off Pinny's head.

What was that about my head?!

▶ *Time to cut.* Don't be nervous, and take your time. It's best to cut standing over the table, keeping the bottom edge of the scissors and the fabric touching the table as much as possible. The more pins used, the more stable and easier cutting will be. Don't lift the fabric in the air or let part of it drape off the table, especially if the fabric is stretchy. If you cut correctly, the fabric pieces will look just like the pattern pieces.

The pieces are cut out. Can we start sewing now?

▶ *Slow down there, eager beaver.* Before you unpin the paper, the pattern pieces need to be checked for marks. Use your detective eyes to find any unusual marks:

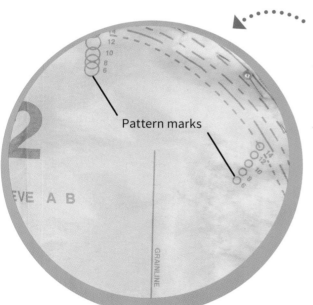

Pattern marks

These marks can be circles or triangles and will be used to match the piece to other areas of the garment for placement. If you find one, transfer the mark to the corresponding fabric piece. You only have to transfer the mark for your size, but if there's no size number listed next to it, then assume the mark is for all sizes.

Grab a fabric marker or chalk. Wherever there is a mark, put a straight pin through it and into the fabric, straight down. Carefully, lift the pattern up and mark where the straight pin is piercing the fabric. If there are two fabric pieces, mark both of them. I prefer marking the wrong side of the fabric, but it's okay to do it on the right side too.

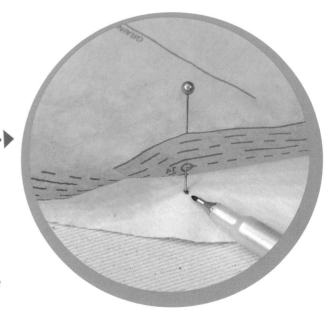

And if you're wondering, "Can we finally sew?"—the answer is yes. With the pattern prep work done, the sewing fun can begin.

Chapter Eight
Pajama Shorts

I don't think we're ever going to sew clothes in this book.

▶ *Did you not look at the chapter name?*
We're going to do it right now.

Wait! I'm actually not ready!

▶ *In my professional opinion, you are ready.*

Photo by Allison Clarke

PROJECT TIME
Pajama Shorts

In this lesson, you'll create some comfortable pajama shorts from scratch. You'll learn how to:

▶ match notches

▶ use a seam ripper

▶ sew a curved seam

▶ sew a machine basting stitch

▶ create an elastic waistband

▶ hem

FABRIC

Flannel or quilter's cotton

FABRIC REQUIREMENTS

Hip Measurement	31½″ (80cm)	33½″ (85cm)	36″ (92cm)	40″ (102cm)	44″ (112cm)	48″ (122cm)
Size	XS (4–6)	S (8–10)	M (12–14)	L (16–18)	XL (20–22)	XXL (24–26)
Fabric Amount 44″ (112cm) Width	1 yard (.92m)	1⅛ yds (1.1m)	1⅛ yds (1.1m)	1¼ yds (1.2m)	1¼ yds (1.2m)	1¼ yds (1.2m)

NOTIONS

All-purpose thread

1 package of 1″ (2.5cm)-wide elastic

TOOLS

Sewing machine

Straight pins

Safety pin

Sewing gauge

Scissors

Universal or sharp sewing machine needle, size 80/12

Iron and ironing board

Preparing the Fabric

STEP 1 If you didn't do it earlier, download and print your pattern pieces:

Scan this QR code or visit tinyurl.com/11504-pattern2-download to download the pattern. Do not print from your phone.

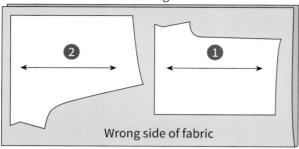

Selvage

Wrong side of fabric

Fold

Cut out your pattern pieces and pin them to your fabric using this layout: •••••••••

After everything is pinned, cut out the fabric pieces. There are two pattern pieces: **Shorts Front ❶** and **Shorts Back ❷**. Because you folded the fabric, you should end up with two fabric pieces from each pattern piece that are mirror images of each other. This means there's a left side and a right side of **Shorts Front** and a left side and right side of **Shorts Back**. Make sure to cut your notches!

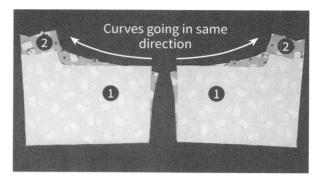

Curves going in same direction

STEP 2 It's time to match the two sets of **Shorts Front ❶** and **Shorts Back ❷** with their correct partners. How do you know which two go together? When placed with the right sides of the fabric together, the curves should go in the same direction. If they go in opposite directions, swap pairings.

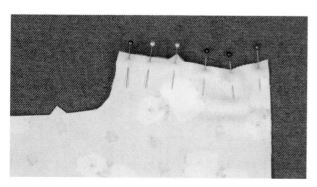

STEP 3 On each pair, match the short edges together. This will be the inner leg seam.

Pin this edge. When pinning fabric for sewing, put the straight pins perpendicular to the fabric's edge to make it easier to remove while sewing. This is not to be confused with pinning pieces for pattern cutting, when pins should be parallel to the pattern edge.

Starting point for easing

When pinning seams, it's best to use a technique called *easing*. It seems natural to start pinning at one end and work toward the other end, but if you do this, you might finish with edges that aren't matching up. To avoid this, start by putting a pin at each end of the area you're pinning and at any other major points (like notches). Then continue placing them evenly between the existing pins, making the gaps between pins smaller and smaller. This will ensure that you're pinning both pieces evenly.

Starting to Sew

STEP 4 It's time to go to the sewing machine. But first, let's do the sewing machine checklist:

▶ Insert a universal or sharp needle, size 80/12.

▶ Set the stitch length to 2.5.

▶ Set the stitch width to 0.

▶ Set the thread tension to 4.

▶ Use a standard sewing machine foot.

I'm ready!

▶ *Sew the inner leg seams you just pinned* with a ⅝″ (1.6cm) seam allowance on both pairs. Don't forget to backstitch at the beginning and end so the stitches don't come out.

Break Time: I Don't Like My Seam!

My seam is ugly! I want a do-over!

▶ *In sewing, do-overs are allowed.* Grab a seam ripper. Put the seam ripper point under the first stitch on one side of the seam and slide to the curved section of the blade to cut the thread. Repeat this process every four or five stitches for the whole length of the seam. **A**

Flip the fabric over to see the stitches on the other side. Use the seam ripper point to pull the thread up, and it should come apart. If it doesn't come out easily, break more stitches on the front. Remove all thread strands to clean the area. **B**

Now you can try that seam again.

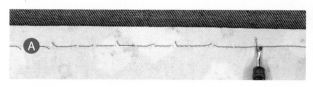

Pressing the Fabric

STEP 5 Heat up your iron because it's time to press.

Usually, irons have adjustable heat settings, and you should choose a setting based on the fabric content. Because these pajama shorts are being made from fabric that's 100% cotton, choose the cotton setting, which is a high heat.

Take your pieces to the ironing board, and, looking at the wrong side of the fabric, spread pieces 1 and 2 apart so the seam is in the middle. Open and flatten the seam allowance, placing the iron down for a few seconds, repeating until the whole seam allowance is pressed flat to either side.

This is called **pressing a seam open**. Don't slide the iron across the fabric; instead, lift the iron up and put it down. This technique prevents the fabric from distorting or stretching. Sometimes seams should be pressed open, and sometimes the directions indicate they should stay together and pressed to one side. Either way, pressing after sewing a seam is a great idea to keep things accurate and neat.

Continuing to Sew

STEP 6 There are now two separate pieces with their inner leg seams stitched. Lay the pieces on top of each other, right sides together. See the curved sections with the single and double notches? These are the crotch curves. In this case, the single notches indicate the front of the garment and the double indicate the back. Line the crotch curves up, using straight pins to hold them together. Match the edges, notches, and the inner leg seams.

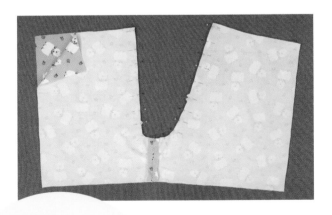

STEP 7 Sew the crotch curve on your machine with a ⅝″ (1.6cm) seam allowance.

TIP
Unless commercial patterns specifically indicate something different, ⅝″ will be your standard seam allowance.

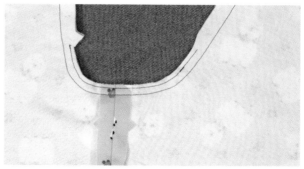

If you're veering off the path while sewing the curve, stop sewing and put the needle into the fabric using the handwheel. Lift the presser foot and adjust the fabric for a more accurate seam allowance. Then put the presser foot down and start sewing again. You can do it.

STEP 8 The center of the crotch curve will get the most wear and tear, so this area needs to be reinforced.

To do this, add a second row of stitches to the center of the curve. Take the shorts back to the sewing machine, and sew the curve seam again, this time at a ⅜″ (1cm) seam allowance. Afterward, trim the seam allowance, only where there are two rows of stitches, to remove some of the bulk and make the shorts more comfortable to wear. Don't cut too close to the stitches. Then press your seam allowance open as much as you can.

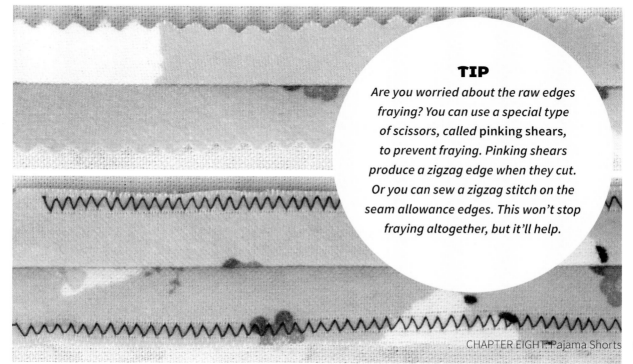

TIP

Are you worried about the raw edges fraying? You can use a special type of scissors, called **pinking shears,** *to prevent fraying. Pinking shears produce a zigzag edge when they cut. Or you can sew a zigzag stitch on the seam allowance edges. This won't stop fraying altogether, but it'll help.*

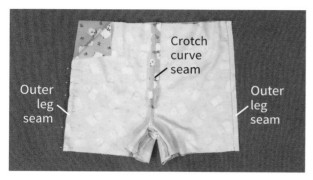

STEP 9 Take the ends of the crotch curve seams and bring them together, keeping the right sides of the fabric together. The unsewn edges on the left and right are the outer leg seams. Pin each side, sew a standard seam, and press the seams open.

STEP 10 At the top of the shorts, there are four seam allowances: the front and back of the crotch curve and the two outer leg seams. So, you're going to sew a **machine basting stitch** to hold those seam allowances open.

A basting stitch is a temporary stitch that helps make some part of the process easier and is later removed. It's a straight stitch with a longer stitch length and no backstitching. In this case, it helps ensure that the elastic will run smoothly through the waistline casing. If the seam allowances are not basted, the elastic might get stuck, which can lead to crying. This car is taking a detour from Crying Avenue.

Change the stitch length on your sewing machine to the highest number. On my machine, this is a 5. Sew each side of all the open waistline seam allowances about 3″ (7.6cm) down. Don't backstitch because these stitches will eventually be removed. Only sew through the seam allowance and the fabric directly beneath it. Don't accidentally sew the waistline shut!

But wait—why are they so big? Are my shorts going to fall down? This is not the kind of sewing magic I want!

▶ *This is where elastic comes to the rescue.* The waistline needs to expand in order to be pulled over the hips and backside. That's why the shorts look big now. Elastic was used to gather the hair scrunchie, and the same thing will happen with the top of our shorts.

Sewing the Elastic Casing

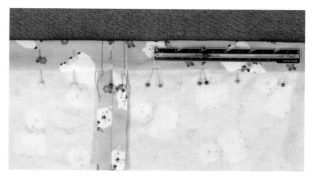

STEP 11 Time to create the elastic casing. The shorts are still wrong side out. Fold 1½″ (3.8cm) of the top of the shorts to the wrong side around the whole waistline circumference, putting in pins to hold. When easing, always pin the seam allowance areas first, and then pin the areas in between. Press with the iron to create a nice crease in the fabric all the way around the waistline.

Next, tuck the bottom raw edge under by ¼″ (6mm). The casing size becomes 1¼″ (3.2cm). The elastic width is 1″ (2.5cm), so the casing is slightly larger to ensure that the elastic will fit. Repin and press the casing again.

Use straight pins to make two X's about 2″ (5cm) apart, anywhere between the seam allowances. Just like with the scrunchie, this creates a gap for inserting the elastic.

- -

STEP 12 On the machine, start sewing at one X, continue around the entire waistline, and stop at the second X (don't stitch between the X's). Stitch close to the bottom folded edge. Take your time and don't forget to backstitch.

Wait!
What's your stitch length?

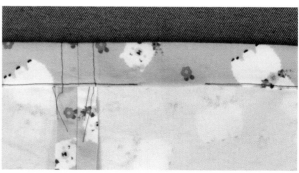

▶ *Good catch, Pinny.* The last thing you did at the sewing machine was a basting stitch. Don't forget to do the sewing machine checklist. This stitch should be a standard straight stitch, at a stitch length of 2.5.

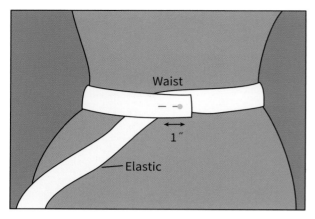

STEP 13 Break out the elastic. Take one end of the elastic and wrap it around your waist, overlapping the ends by 1″ (2.5cm). It should fit snugly. Cut off the excess elastic, overlap the ends again, and pin them.

STEP 14 Put a safety pin on one end of the elastic. Just like in the scrunchie project, the safety pin helps you pull the elastic through the casing.

I'm getting good at this.

▶ *See? Basic techniques start to get familiar.* Remember, you don't want the other end of the elastic to get pulled into the casing, so pin one end of the elastic to the outside.

As the elastic goes through, the casing will gather. When the elastic ends are together again, overlap them by 1″ (2.5cm) and pin. If you want to try on your shorts to make sure the elastic feels good, you can.

Then, pull the overlapped elastic section away from the casing and stitch the elastic ends together. Because this elastic is wider, stitch in a box shape for extra security.

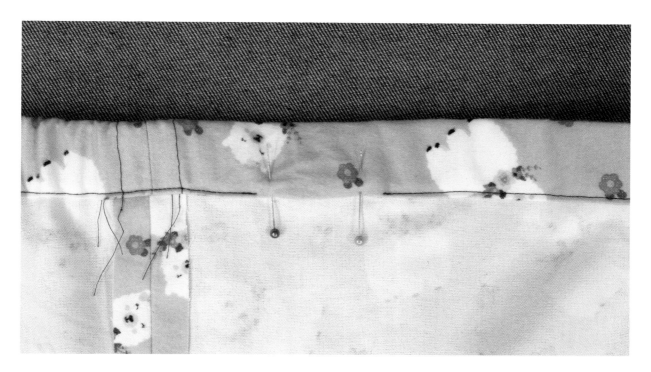

STEP 15 Stretch the waistline until all of the elastic is inside the casing, then pin the fabric gap closed.

Sew a standard straight stitch along the bottom folded edge to close the opening. Then evenly distribute the gathered fabric along the waistline.

Phew!
Are we
done now?

▶ *Almost. There's still the hem.*

Sewing the Hem

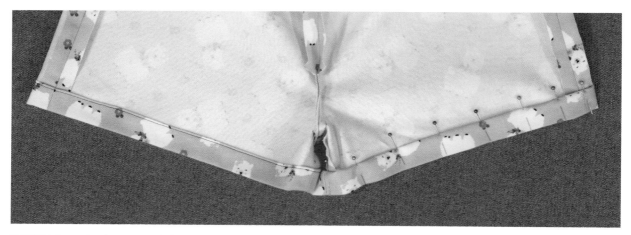

STEP 16 At the bottom of the shorts, fold up 1¼″ (3.2cm) all the way around each leg to the wrong side of the fabric. Pin and press. Tuck the top raw edge under by ¼″ (6mm) so the folded section will now measure 1″ (2.5cm). Pin and press again. Then, stitch at the top folded edge. Each leg now has a nice hem.

STEP 17 The only thing remaining is to give your garment a final look over. Remove any loose threads, take out those casing basting stitches with a seam ripper, and give the garment a nice, final press if there are any visible wrinkles.

Flip those shorts right side out and … voilà!
You made your own pajama shorts. I recommend putting them on straightaway and strutting confidently to bed because you earned yourself a nap after a job well done. ••••••••••••••••➤

If you want to try your hand at a similar commercial pattern or would prefer pajama pants, you can try these:

Images courtesy of SIMPLICITY® (or McCall's®) by Design Group America

Chapter Nine
T-Shirt

By now, your whole family, all your friends, and your neighbors know that you've made a pair of pajama shorts because it's really hard not to show and tell.

I wonder if my whole wardrobe can be pajama shorts?

▶ *Before you start cutting more flannel, let's try a different project.* It's time to tackle a T-shirt, which will help you get more comfortable sewing with knit fabric.

PROJECT TIME
T-Shirt

We're going to create a basic T-shirt from a pattern. You'll learn how to:

▶ work with knit   ▶ sew in a neckband   ▶ sew curved hemlines

▶ baste to ease   ▶ sew a sleeve

FABRIC

Cotton interlock or jersey knit

FABRIC REQUIREMENTS

Bust/Chest Measurement	29½″ (75cm)	31½″ (80cm)	34″ (87cm)	38″ (97cm)	42″ (107cm)	46″ (117cm)
Waist Measurement	22″ (56cm)	24″ (61cm)	26½″ (67cm)	30″ (76cm)	34″ (87cm)	39″ (99cm)
Sizes	XS (4–6)	S (8–10)	M (12–14)	L (16–18)	XL (20–22)	XXL (24–26)
Fabric Amount 58″/60″ (148/150cm) width	1⅛ yard (1.1m)	1⅛ yard (1.1m)	1⅛ yard (1.1m)	1¼ yds (1.2m)	1¼ yds (1.2m)	1⅓ yds (1.3m)

NOTIONS

All-purpose thread

TOOLS

Sewing machine

Straight pins

Sewing gauge

Scissors

Ballpoint sewing machine needle, size 80/12

Iron and ironing board

Preparing the Fabric

STEP 1 Download and print your pattern pieces:

Scan this QR code or visit tinyurl.com/11504-pattern3-download to download the pattern. Do not print from your phone.

Cut out your pattern pieces and pin them to your fabric using this layout:

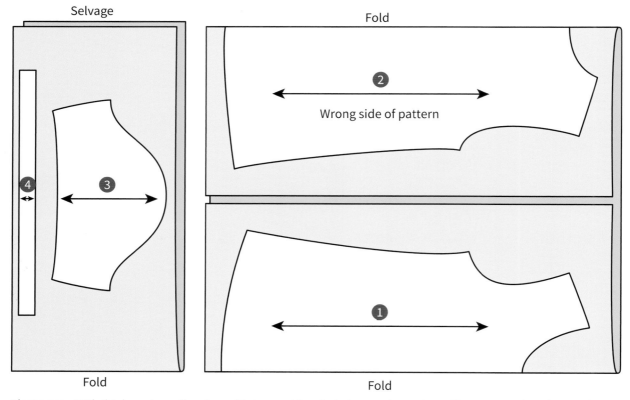

Please note: With this layout, you'll end up with two neckbands, but you only need one. You can toss the other.

Be careful when cutting knit fabric. Place the knit completely flat on the table, so gravity doesn't pull or distort pieces as you cut. Avoid lifting the fabric as much as possible.

There are four pattern pieces: **T-shirt Front 1**, **T-shirt Back 2**, **Sleeve 3**, and **Neckband 4**. This layout is different from the shorts layout in that two pieces need to be cut on a fold (1 and 2). You'll need two sleeves (a left and right) and one neckband. Cut out the fabric pieces.

TIP
Some knit edges will curl, which is a massive headache. If this happens, and the fabric is washable, spray the fabric with spray starch to stiffen it and make it easier to work with. Then wash it out when the garment is finished.

Are you ignoring that mark on the sleeve pattern?

▶ *That mark is needed to match the sleeve to the armhole.* Mark it on your fabric pieces.

Break Time: Sleeves

How are the right and left sleeves different? They look the same to me.

▶ *Sleeve pieces are not perfectly symmetrical.* The back of the sleeve is usually bigger than the front because most people need more room there. On the curved edge of the sleeve cap, one side has a single notch and one side has a double notch. As we learned in the pajama shorts section, these notches can differentiate between the front and back of the pattern. The side with the single notch is the sleeve front and the side with the double notch is the sleeve back. If the pattern is cut on folded fabric, as recommended in the layout, you'll automatically get the exact sleeves you need.

Starting to Sew

STEP 2 Time to go through our sewing machine checklist:

▶ Insert ballpoint needle, size 80/12.

▶ Set the stitch length to 2.5.

▶ Set the stitch width to 0.

▶ Set the thread tension to 4.

▶ Use a standard sewing machine foot.

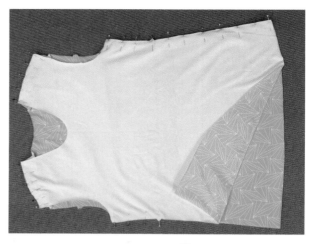

TIP

Don't be afraid to test the machine settings on scraps of knit fabric until both stitches and fabric look good; adjust the thread tension dial if necessary. Learn what your sewing machine likes. This can vary from fabric to fabric. If the seam is wavy, decrease the thread tension. The ideal stitch looks the same on the front and back, and the seam should lie flat.

STEP 3 Place **T-shirt Front** ❶ and **T-shirt Back** ❷ together, right sides touching, and match the shoulder and side seams. Then, use the easing method to pin all four seams.

You should know what to do now.

Take it to the sewing machine?

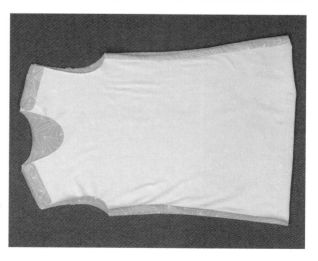

▶ *Using a standard seam allowance* of ⅝″ (1.6cm), sew the four seams. Don't forget to backstitch at the beginning and end of each seam. Press each seam open. Check the iron, making sure it's set to the right heat setting for the fabric type.

Sleeves

STEP 4 At this point, you have a tank top. Let's add sleeves! First, prep the machine for basting stitches. Remember those? Head back to Chapter Eight, Step 10 (page 86) if not. This will help you fit the sleeve into the armhole.

For each sleeve, sew two rows of basting stitches from notch to notch, one stitch at ⅝″ (1.6cm) and one at the ½″ (1.2cm) seamline. These basting stitches will eventually be pulled to cinch the sleeves and fit them into the armholes. Having two rows helps ensure that the basting stitches won't break when pulled.

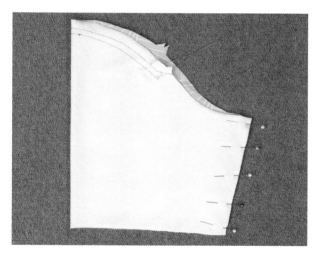

STEP 5 The underarm seam is on the underside of each sleeve. Bring the short two edges together (with right sides touching) and pin. Sew a standard seam and press it open. Do the same for the second sleeve.

STEP 6 Now it's time to hem the sleeves. This will be similar to the pajama shorts hem. With the sleeves still wrong side out, fold the bottom straight edge 1¼″ (3.2cm). Pin and press. Turn the top edge under by ¼″ (6mm), making the folded area 1″ (2.5cm). Pin and press again.

Sometimes, the accessory box can be removed from the sewing machine base, making the base narrower. This helps when sewing items like sleeves. Not all sewing machines have this removable option, but remove the extra piece if your machine does.

Sew the top folded edge with either a longer stitch length, like a 3.5, or change the stitch width to a 2 to create a narrow zigzag stitch. This will allow the hem to retain some stretchiness. Do the same to the second sleeve.

STEP 7 Ready to put in the sleeves? First, the correct sleeve needs to go in the correct armhole.

Oh yeah, there's a right sleeve and a left sleeve.

▶ *Now you're getting it.* The tank top should be wrong side out and the sleeves should be right side out. Put a sleeve inside an armhole, hem in first. Before you do any pinning, look at the notches. With the sleeve underarm seam and the T-shirt side seam lined up, the single notches and the double notches on the sleeve and T-shirt armhole should match.

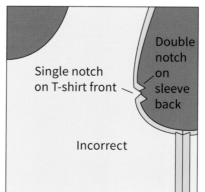

Single notch on T-shirt front — Double notch on sleeve back

Incorrect

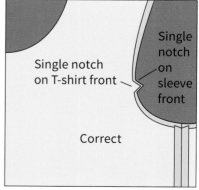

Single notch on T-shirt front — Single notch on sleeve front

Correct

Oh no! Mine doesn't match! Have I messed up?

▶ *No.* Instead, try the sleeve in the other armhole. If they did match, congratulations on getting it right the first time.

Here's what mine looks like: ••••▶

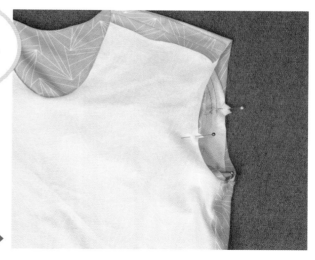

Pin at the seam and notches. The top center mark on the sleeve matches with the shirt's shoulder seam. But as you start to pin the area in between, it may seem like there's too much sleeve material to fit inside the armhole.

Don't panic. Remember sewing those two rows of basting stitches? Gently pull on both thread tails and the sleeve fabric will start to cinch. It's easing the fabric to fit.

But beware: If you pull too much, it'll be less easing and more gathering (or creating ruffles).

▶ *You don't want the top of the T-shirt sleeves to look ruffled. Pull only a little and distribute the gathered fabric along the sleeve, so it's slightly wavy.*

Once it's been eased enough to fit, pin the sleeve to the armhole all the way around.

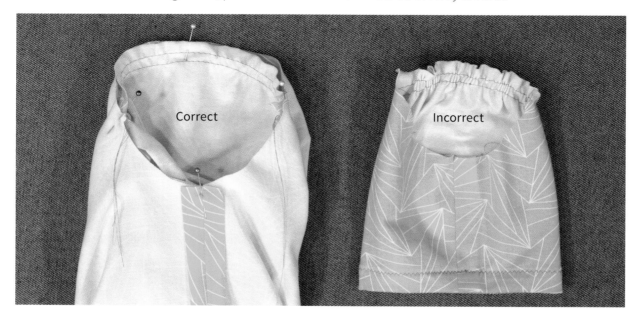

It's starting to look like a real T-shirt now.

STEP 8 Take the shirt to the machine and sew a ⅝″ (1.6cm) standard seam around each sleeve. I like to feel the area while sewing to make sure I'm not accidentally sewing a wrinkle into the seam.

After the sleeve is sewed in, turn the T-shirt right side out to inspect it. Are there any wrinkles? Does the seam ripper need to be broken out? Sometimes tiny wrinkles can be massaged out. Try this before taking a seam ripper to it.

STEP 9 When it comes to T-shirts, most wear and tear happens to the bottom of the armhole due to natural movement. To strengthen this area, turn the shirt inside out again and do another row of stitches at the bottom of the armhole, from single notch to double notch, at the ½″ (1.2cm) line. After this, trim the seam allowance to cut down on bulk, but don't cut the stitches.

With one sleeve sewn in, repeat the process for the other one.

The Neckband

STEP 10 There's still one more pattern piece that hasn't been used.

The Neck Band! I like their music!

▶ **What?** No, the neckband has nothing to do with music. This is a strip of fabric used to finish the neckline. Take the neckband fabric and pin the short ends together. Sew a standard seam and press.

The neckband is now a loop. Fold the fabric in half widthwise with wrong sides together and press with an iron to create a crease at the fold.

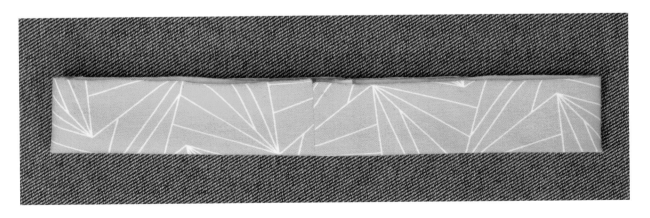

There's no way this neckband is going to fit on this T-shirt. It's too small.

▶ *This is normal; in fact, it should be small so it will lie flat when it's finished.*

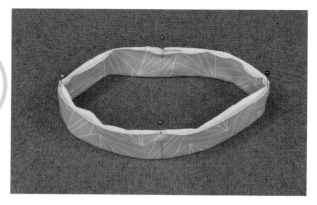

STEP 11 Flatten the neckband with the seam in the center. Put a pin on the raw edges at the neckband's seam, then put another pin directly opposite. Add two more pins to the left and right folds. There are now four pins in the neckband at an equal distance from each other, dividing it into quarters.

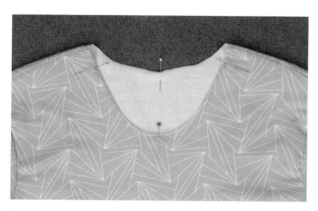

Repeat this same process with the T-shirt neckline. Fold the T-shirt in half by bringing the shoulder seams together and put a pin at the center back and center front. Then bring those pins together to find the left and right centers.

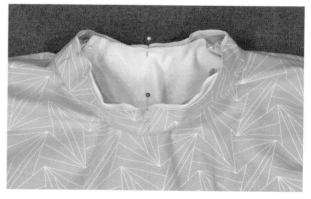

STEP 12 Pin the neckband to the neckline on the right side of the T-shirt, matching pin to pin, with the raw edges lined up. Match the neckband seam with the T-shirt's center back pin so the seam is on the back of the shirt. You can add pins in between the four, but don't add too many because you'll be stretching the neckband as you sew.

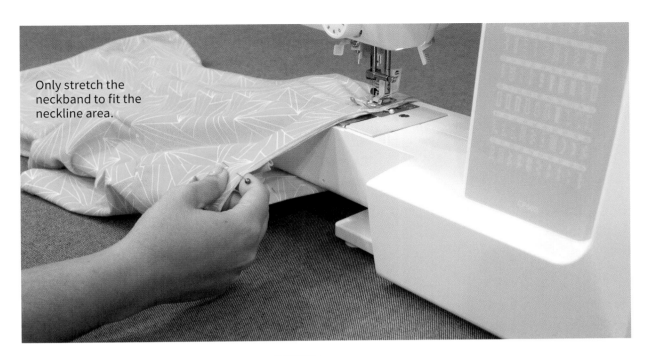

Only stretch the neckband to fit the neckline area.

STEP 13 Remember when I said we don't want to stretch our knit fabric?

Yeah, you said never stretch.

▶ *Well, I never say* **never.** Because there's always a sometimes. Guess what? This is one of those sometimes moments. Enjoy it.

At the sewing machine, start at one pin. Sew a standard seam, stretching the neckband to fit the area of the neckline between the pins. Repeat, stretching and sewing between the next pair of the pins. Keep doing this all the way around the neckline. Use a straight stitch with a stitch length of 3.5, or do a narrow zigzag stitch to allow some stretch in the neckline, just like with the sleeve hemline.

STEP 14 After the neckband is in, check the right side of the seamline to make sure there aren't any unsightly wrinkles. If it's smooth, trim the seam allowance, being careful not to cut any stitches, and then press the neckband upward. Remember you can always reach for the seam ripper if you want to try again, but keep in mind that seam do-overs must happen before you trim away seam allowances.

STEP 15 Finally, there's the bottom hem. The T-shirt front has a curved hem and the back has a straight hem. Curved hemlines are a little more complex than straight ones because they need to be eased into place. Machine baste ¼″ (6mm) away from the bottom raw edge on the curved front portion.

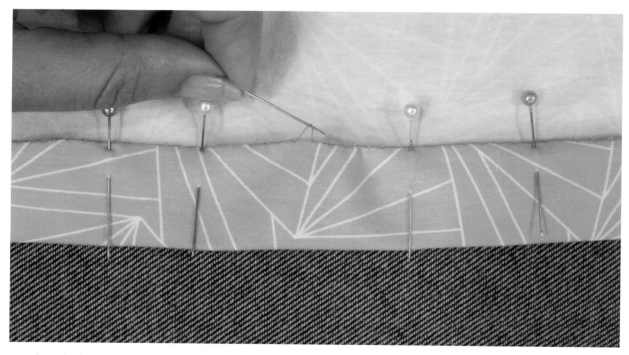

For the whole bottom edge of the T-shirt, fold 1¼″ (3.2cm) to the wrong side and press. Then turn the raw edge under by ¼″ (6mm) and press again. On the curved section, if the hem isn't fitting (which happens because the outer part of a curve is bigger than the inner part of a curve), gently use a straight pin to pull the basting stitches and cinch the fabric in the ill-fitting section until it fits.

Now stitch to victory at the machine with a narrow zigzag or longer straight stitch.

Did you still end up with a wavy seam or hem somewhere?

Yes! Should I throw the whole thing in the trash?

TIP

Before you get steamed, consider using some steam. Here's a little trick for wavy necklines or hems. Make sure there is water in the iron's water reserve. Put the iron on a high heat setting and hover it over the affected (wavy) area of the garment. Press the steam button on the iron to get the fabric good and steamy. This helps shrink the area, making it less wavy.

STEP 16 Before you wear the T-shirt, look over it. Remove any loose threads and any visible basting stitches. Does it need a final press? You've already done this much work, no reason to skimp at the end.

Another project done

▶ *Good job, newbies. Pinny and I are proud of you.*

If you want to try your hand at a similar commercial pattern or would prefer longer sleeves, you can try these:

Images courtesy of SIMPLICITY® by Design Group Americas

Chapter Ten
Conclusion

Wait? This is the last chapter? Have we learned everything about sewing?

▶ **Everything about sewing?** No, not even close. There's still a lot to learn, like zippers and buttonholes and waistbands and collars.

But I'm still nervous! How will I do it?

▶ **It's okay to be nervous.** You're going to do what you've done throughout this whole book: Take it one step at a time. One thing I've learned is to not try to understand everything at once. It's overwhelming, and then I get anxious. Instead, focus on one step before worrying about the next. Sometimes things that don't seem clear at the beginning become clearer later.

If you continue picking patterns labeled "easy," you'll begin to pick up more skills. And don't forget that commercial patterns include their own set of pattern directions: •••••••••••••••••••••••►

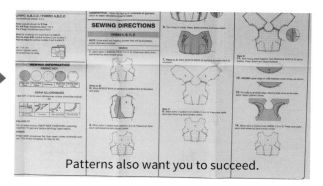

Patterns also want you to succeed.

Patterns include step-by-step written instructions and illustrations. As long as you can follow directions, you'll find yourself sewing lots of garments that you can show off to friends, family members, and even continually impressed goldfish.

And if you do get stuck, remember that there are a ton of resources out there to help you, like Professor Pincushion (professorpincushion.com). You can type "how to sew in a zipper" into the search engine and find several videos, or blog posts, that will show you exactly how to sew one in.

Learning to sew is actually learning to be brave. It's jumping in and trying something new. You may mess up, you may not get it the first time around, but doing it is the best way to learn. If you're really unsure, do a test run. Buy cheaper fabric, like muslin or something similar, and go through the directions. This will give you a preview of how it's done, and then you can make the final garment with more expensive fabric. This isn't unusual; many people make a "muslin" to test patterns and fit.

Have fun with it, though. Take pictures in order to keep track of your progress. Your projects will get more complex as you gain the confidence to try new things.

The real motivation for leveling up your sewing XP is being inspired by a pattern or fabric or your own imagination.

And where we're going, we don't need pins.

▶ *Please continue to use all the tools, including straight pins.* They'll be there for you when you get that sewing inspiration. Go for it! You can do it! And don't forget that Pinny and I are behind you all the way, cheering you on. Because this is not the end of your sewing journey. It's just the beginning, brave newbies.

Index

armhole, Ch 9

backstitch, Ch 2, Ch 4

basting, Ch 8, Ch 9

bobbin, Ch 2

  drop-in threading, Ch 2

  front-loading threading, Ch 2

body measurement chart, Ch 6

easing, Ch 8, Ch 9

elastic, Ch 5, Ch 8

elastic waistband, Ch 8

fabric, Ch 1, Ch 3

  choosing fabric, Ch 3

  knit fabric, Ch 3, Ch 4, Ch 9

  pretreating, Ch 7

  right side/wrong side, Ch 3

  widths, Ch 6

  woven fabric, Ch 3, Ch 5, Ch 8

fabric chalk, Ch 1

markings, Ch 7

grainline, Ch 7

handwheel, Ch 2

hem, Ch 8, Ch 9

  iron, Ch 1

  pressing, Ch 8, Ch 9

  steaming, Ch 9

knit, see fabric

lookbooks, Ch 6

neckband, Ch 9

needle, Ch 1, Ch 2, Ch 4, Ch 5

  changing, Ch 2

  hand, Ch 1

  machine, Ch 2, Ch 4

notch, Ch 7, Ch 8

notions, Ch 1, Ch 6

pajama shorts, Ch 8

  basting, Ch 8

  crotch curve, Ch 8

  elastic, Ch 8

  hem, Ch 8

  waistband casing, Ch 8

pattern, Ch 6, Ch 7

  choosing a pattern, Ch 6

  cutting, Ch 7

  downloadable, Ch 7

  fabric amount, Ch 6

  fabric recommendation, Ch 6

  finished garment measurement, Ch 6

  grainline, Ch 7

  layout, Ch 7

  markings, Ch 7

  measurement chart, Ch 6

  notions, Ch 6

  notches, Ch 7

  pattern envelope, Ch 6

  right side/wrong side, Ch 7

  sizing, Ch 6

pincushion, Ch 1

presser foot, Ch 2

Changing, Ch 2

pressing, Ch 8, Ch 9

running stitch, Ch 5

reverse stitch, Ch 2, Ch 4

scissors, Ch 1

pinking shears, Ch 8

scrunchie, Ch 5

seam, Ch 5

  allowance, Ch 5

  curved, Ch 8

  finishing, Ch 8

  pressing, Ch 8

  removing, Ch 8

  trimming, Ch 8, Ch 9

seam ripper, Ch 1

  using, Ch 8

sewing gauge, Ch 1

  breakdown, Ch 6

sewing machine, Ch 2

  bobbin, Ch 2

  drop-in threading, Ch 2

  front-loading threading, Ch 2

  feed dogs, Ch 2

  handwheel, Ch 2

  presser foot, Ch 2

  changing, Ch 2

  needle plate, Ch 2

  needles, Ch 2

  changing, Ch 2

  sizing, Ch 4

  safety, Ch 2

  stitch length, Ch 2

stitch selector, Ch 2

stitch width, Ch 2

threading, Ch 2

thread tension, Ch 2, Ch 9

sleeve, Ch 9

slip stitch, Ch 5

stitch length, Ch 2

stitch selector, Ch 2

stitch width, Ch 2

straight pin, Ch 1

pinning patterns, Ch 7

pinning seams, Ch 5, Ch 8

tape measure, flexible, Ch 1

  breakdown, Ch 6

  measuring, Ch 6

thread, Ch 1

threading, Ch 2

thread tension, Ch 2, Ch 9

T-shirt, Ch 4, Ch 9

  armhole, Ch 9

  alterations, Ch 4

  basting, Ch 9

  bag, Ch 4

  easing, Ch 9

  hem, Ch 9

  neckband, Ch 9

  sleeve, Ch 9

woven, *see fabric*

zigzag stitch, Ch 5

About the Author

Tova Opatrny sewed her first hair scrunchie in high school and has been at the sewing machine ever since. In 2009, she cofounded the website and YouTube channel Professor Pincushion in order to produce high-quality video tutorials for beginners. Tova's work has appeared in *Huffpost*, *Good Housekeeping*, and *Cosmopolitan*, among others. She currently resides in central Oregon with her husband and their cat, Hitchcock, and dog, Pippin. She has never stepped on a straight pin in her life.

Lookin' good, Professor! *
She made me say that.